Twentieth Century Anglo-Welsh Poetry

Twentieth Century Anglo-Welsh Poetry

Edited by
Dannie Abse

seren

seren is the book imprint of
Poetry Wales Press Ltd,
Wyndham Street, Bridgend,
CF31 1EF, Wales

Introduction & Editorial © Dannie Abse, 1997
For individual contributions see Acknowledgements pages

ISBN: 1-85411-182-5
1-85411-183-3 paperback

A CIP record for this title is available from
the British Library

*The publisher acknowledges the financial support
of the Arts Council of Wales*

Cover illustration: 'Blue Rectangle' by Rachel Windham

Printed in Plantin by
Cromwell Press, Melksham, Wiltshire

CONTENTS

INTRODUCTION

During the twentieth century, until recently, the Welsh language remained in retreat in much of Wales. Yet despite the loss of language the old cultural particularities were partly sustained. Spoken English itself was, and continues to be, Welsh-pollinated and the contribution to English literature has burgeoned.

What characterises the English language poetry written by Welsh men and women? I fear that in 1960, during a BBC broadcast, I suggested, negatively, that a poem with the appellation of 'Sunday Evening' would be endorsed as an Anglo-Welsh poem simply by the ruse of retitling it 'Sunday Evening in Ystrad Mynach'. I argued that "We should beware of Anglo-Welsh mongering and recognise typographical fraud for what it is ... that a poem about a magpie seen in Wales is no different basically from a poem about a magpie seen in England and a love poem is unlikely, generally, to have a Welsh connotation if written in English by a Welshman. To put it in another way; there is no such thing as a specific Anglo-Welsh style or tone, and the Welshness of an English poem simply depends on what the poem is about."

These early remarks of mine, I now realise, portray only part of the truth and are deficient in complexity as the multiplicity of the comments of knowledgeable critics anthologised in the Prologue that follows surely demonstrate. Indeed, if generalisations are permitted, further characteristics of Anglo-Welsh poetry could be listed which are not mentioned in the Prologue. For instance, it is evident that many poets in Wales, rightly or wrongly, believe themselves to be members of a defeated nation. That awareness leads them, in the signature of their poems, to side with the losers of history and of life's procession — the underdogs, the outsiders, the downtrodden. And the poems, themselves, whether or not touching on such themes, not infrequently aim at the tropopause of feeling. Robert Browning's, 'O my dove, let us be unashamed of soul,' would have been, in the main, a needless imperative if addressed to the poets of Wales.

Anglo-Welsh poems had, by the 1930s, become distinctive enough for writers such as Dylan Thomas to wish that a literary magazine existed that would publish Welsh-flavoured poems and prose. In October 1933, Thomas, addressing a letter to Trevor Hughes, spoke of starting a magazine himself, one which would own a recognisable Welsh pulse-beat. Though that dreamed-of periodical never materialised two others did before the decade closed: *Wales*, edited by Keidrich Rhys and *The Welsh Review*, edited by Gwyn Jones. In 1938, Dylan Thomas attempted to persuade the BBC "to broadcast a short series of readings by Welsh poets or poets of Welsh ancestry who wrote in English: from Vaughan to Edward Thomas, Wilfred Owen, W.H. Davies and the younger men, contributors to the periodical *Wales* and to most of the periodicals published in London and abroad who are now making what is really a renaissance of Welsh writing."

Meanwhile Dylan Thomas did not feel Keidrich Rhys's *Wales* to be Welsh-centred enough. He ranted, "You (Rhys) have dragged into your magazine all the little waste names ... that belong to London rags and not in thought or feeling, to anything connected with Wales." Six years later, after that surprising castigation, Keidrich Rhys tried to put Anglo-Welsh poetry 'on the map' by editing an anthology for Faber entitled, *Modern Welsh Poetry*. Though Idris Davies, Glyn Jones, Alun Lewis, Dylan Thomas, R.S. Thomas and Vernon Watkins were included, the anthology was too diluted by dud pieces to make a permanent mark.

A second flowering of twentieth century Anglo-Welsh poetry in the 1960s, partly rooted in Welsh nationalism, had to come into being before anthologists tried once more to draw attention to at least one half of Wales's poetry phantascope. Amongst the most notable were *Welsh Voices* (Dent), edited by Bryn Griffiths, 1967; *The Lilting House* (Dent), edited by John Stuart Williams and Meic Stephens, 1969; and *Anglo-Welsh Poetry 1430-1980* (Seren), updated in its second impression, edited by Raymond Garlick and Roland Mathias.

Despite anthologies such as these, despite lively literary magazines in Wales promoted by the Welsh Arts Council, despite the increasingly confident emergence of such Welsh-based publishers as Seren and Gomer, the twentieth century efflorescence of Anglo-Welsh poetry, at English Headquarters and elsewhere, remained something of a secret. As the American, David T. Lloyd has remarked in the Chicago publication *The Urgency of Identity* (TriQuarterly Books, 1994), "This impressive literary awakening is all the more dramatic because of it being scarcely noticed — much less celebrated or studied — outside the borders of Wales."

This present anthology of twentieth century Anglo-Welsh poetry attempts to present samples of that awakening by the best poets of Welsh affiliation writing in English. Readers are likely to discover that these poems prove to be accessible for, generally, the

Welsh poet with his sense of community, while recognising that the language of poetry differs from the language of logic, acknowledges his or her duty to communicate person to person. Those verses imbued with the most *blatant* nationalist valency do not find, for the most part, a place here because platform poems of whatever orientation rarely outlast their season.

Though mindful of previous Anglo-Welsh compilations I have, thanks to the resources of the Arts Council Library in London, been able, over the last two years, to examine innumerable individual volumes in addition to reading again, at home, many books of poems, long owned, long known and long valued. I hope that readers within and beyond the borders of Wales will enjoy what I have enjoyed, what is offered here: reflections of a passing century, war and peace; the celebration of community and locality; the rustic and the urban; the portrayals of people and the articulation of love, grief and anger; the backward look, personal and historical; that which focuses with a bright lens on contemporary Wales and elsewhere; the elegiac and the humorous; all those alert, pleasure-arousing illuminations that the empire of genuine poetry allows, whether signalled from strange Timbuctoo or from the particularity of Llanfihangel-yng-Ngwynfa.

Dannie Abse

PROLOGUE

I have to confess that I have never felt obliged, by virtue of nationality, to seek out an Anglo-Welsh literature which would explain my life and times to me, or celebrate a locality or way-of-life that was recognisably familiar. My primary allegiance has always been to good poetry written in English, regardless of where it comes from; and the human condition in the twentieth century has been desperate enough to render local considerations secondary. And yet. And yet: insofar as we are real flesh and blood, carrying history in our bones, and living in real space and time, then poetry written in a real place and time by writers with a common history will inevitably reflect that reality — and perhaps a common sensibility, too.

Jill Farringdon, 'Confessions of an Anglo-Welsh Reader', *New England Review and Bread Loaf Quarterly*, 1988

The development of an English language poetry in Wales is chiefly a twentieth century phenomenon. It is the natural result of the displacement of Welsh by English as the first, and often the only, language of most Welshmen.

Joseph Clancy, *Twentieth Century Welsh Poems* (Gomer, 1982)

... many Anglo-Welsh poets seem to assume that their function is not primarily to explore the private world of their own thought and feelings but to address their community .... The celebration of particular landscapes, the sense of place, the naming of locations mark many of their poems .... Moreover this sense of place is often associated with a sense of time — sometimes a personal past (as in 'Fern Hill') but more often a national past, the immensely venerable continuity of the history of Wales.

Raymond Garlick and Roland Mathias (eds.), *Anglo-Welsh Poetry 1480-1980* (Poetry Wales Press, 1984)

I see it asserted that the Welsh poet writing in English is doing something different from the English poet, and I can see in an amateur sort of way some of this is so. Whether this is in his craft or in a set of feelings and references is often difficult to separate. I remember the ferocity of the attack of the Movement poets of the '50s on Dylan Thomas, as against that drunken, lurching, word-gas poetry, you know, and what was being pushed in its place was this certainly quite attractive verse of its kind — light social verse — a sort of shrug, polite, carefully not going beyond the emotions of what was probable in almost conversational prose .... And they had ruled out the emotional intensity and the kind of writing that goes with it. I remember being very hostile .... It seemed to me then that Dylan Thomas was not just another English poet.

Raymond Williams Interviewed, *Poetry Wales* 13.3 (1977)

The first batch of twentieth century Anglo-Welsh writers had one strength most of their successors were to be without: they were, if not themselves capable of writing and speaking Welsh, in touch with older members of their own families who spoke the language, and had means of knowing and remembering ... what the Welsh way of life was .... It is possible, too — if now scarcely probable — that the uninhibited eloquence of older Welsh speakers — what is too often loosely called the *hwyl* — had its echo in the extraordinary richness and profusion of language which was common in this first twentieth-century generation of Anglo-Welsh writers.

Roland Mathias, *Anglo-Welsh Literature* (Poetry Wales Press, 1987)

Why do I suggest, then, that a Biblical tone is a Welsh quality? Well, the word *tone* is the key. It is tone, not vocabulary, that suggests Welshness in Dylan (Thomas). And the tone is a preaching tone, a sonorousness of delivery, very occasionally rising to *hwyl*, but never falling to the conversational. It has been suggested that the tone is a manifestation of *bardic impersonality*, but I see little contact with the bardic in Dylan's story. Instead I hear the cadences of the voice of David John Thomas (Dylan's father) as he read the Bible to his young son, the cadences of a man who thought he had cut off his Welsh heritage for good but nevertheless carried ineradicably in his voice-habit the remembrance of the old Welsh preachers of Wales. The Bible was literature, the language often poetry.

Roland Mathias, *A Ride Through the Wood* (Poetry Wales Press, 1985)

Clare Street, in Merthyr, was quite a tidy street when I was born there in 1905. Gradually ... English had become the language of even the town's Welsh speakers, or most of them. English, and only English, was the language of the elementary and grammar schools that I attended. English was the language of the Welsh

Chapel to which I referred earlier, namely Soar Chapel, or at least, while Welsh was the language of the Sunday services, it was English that everyone spoke, whether adults or children, at Sunday School, the concerts, the Band of Hope, the Young People's Meeting and so on. Thus it was that, although Welsh was my parents' first language and that of all their relations in Merthyr and Llansteffan, English gradually became the language of our hearth and our everyday family life. I began speaking English at the age of five, when I first went to school, and I spoke very little Welsh for some twenty years after that.

Glyn Jones, 'The Making of a Poet', *Planet*, 113 (1995)

Quite frankly there seems to be something rather over compensatory in seeking an Anglo-Welsh tradition among the tourists, anglicised gentry and country parsons who dabbled in English verse from Tudor times on. But that is not to say that those poets who made their names during the years 1930-1960 and the new men about us now have not done a great deal to lay the foundations of a tradition that is likely to last .... Only this much is clear: the new poets, with one or two lone wolves to remind us that labels in poetry are so often phoney, all recognise that they have a great deal in common, including a social background, roots if you like, in a particular community.

Meic Stephens, 'The Second Flowering', *Poetry Wales*, 3.3 (1967)

... there are those who fear that the 'Welshness' of many of my compatriots is somehow being seriously drained away, that the old ways, the old religion, the old language, even in the interior of Wales, is being lost now that each house, farmhouse, cottage, sports a television aerial like a twentieth century flag. For instance, where have the righteous orators gone, they ask, the word scriptural or political, intense and thrilling? Gone for the most part, they say, into the photographic plates of a Welsh social history book or into the remembering imaginations of poets. It is not a new complaint. Edward Thomas also uttered how Wales was the locus of the Past. Phantoms, he said, followed phantoms in a phantom land — "a gleam of spears, a murmur of arrows, a shout of victory, a fair face, a scream of torture, a song, the form of some conqueror and pursuer of English Kings". And generations earlier, another poet, Matthew Arnold, visiting nineteenth century Llandudno, remarked that Wales is "where the past still lives, where every place has its tradition, every name its poetry, and where the people, the genuine people, still know this past, this tradition, this poetry, and live with and cling to it."

Are the Welsh 'genuine' people so backward-glancing as these romantic poets, Arnold, Thomas and Thomas, suggest? The more a nation looks to its past the more, paradoxically, that past, that tradition, arrives into the present, vivid and alive. Besides, even when the old customs are sadly mislaid, when the Welsh language itself is lost indisputably, as it is in many regions of Wales, it does not signify that the people of Wales suddenly become Englishmen.

Dannie Abse, *A Strong Dose of Myself* (Hutchinson, 1983)

Anglo-Welsh poets are in general highly conscious of the responsibilities of their position between the Welsh language and culture and the anglicising influences of their medium. Several of them are realising the potentialities of this unique position to create a poetry that is — at least to an English reader — more Welsh than English. By embodying Welshness, English in Wales acquires some of the value of the primary tongue: it becomes more native, more the speech of relationship, and enriches the English language at large by extending its capacity for expressing the life of a distinct culture.

Jeremy Hooker, 'The Poetry of Anthony Conran', *The Anglo-Welsh Review*, 1975

It has been suggested that the younger Anglo-Welsh poets are more Anglo than Welsh because they are not as in touch with the Welsh language as their elders were. According to the 'seepage' theory what distinguished Anglo-Welsh poetry is a style derived from its proximity to Welsh language and literature. Move away from these influences and Anglo-Welsh poetry loses its distinctive qualities.

Is it possible to generalise usefully about older poets like R.S. Thomas, Idris Davies, Alun Lewis and Vernon Watkins? The briefest of examinations reveals how different they are. Many of them were singularly influenced by non-Welsh writers .... It's difficult to generalise about the younger poets, but what they do seem to have in common is a greater radicalism and a stronger sense of the historical and political context of their imaginative worlds than their elders had. Have they been as influenced by non-Welsh writers? Or does this social and political awareness make them more conscious of the force of Welsh language and literature?

Cary Archard, editorial, *Poetry Wales*, 20.1 (1984)

Anglo-Welsh poetry points in no single clear direction, but it does refuse to align itself to the television aerials that point towards the Mendips. That, perhaps, is the best way of putting it. In other words there is an oppositional spirit at work, not because the poets feel distant from some centre but because they feel Wales to be different from elsewhere. It is not a remoteness from London that concerns them but a feeling that Wales is some place other than England, even if their sense of that place is not consistent or clear and even if for some of them its otherness is minimal — the residue of a once clearly separate history. And yet, in spite of the great differences of outlook among them ... contemporary Anglo-Welsh poets would seem to fall into two very broad categories. There are those who conceive of Wales in terms of some alternative society — alternative, that is, to what is commonly perceived as the Anglo-American norm. And there are those whose primarily pragmatic interest in Wales relates more to their appreciation, as artists, of an international modernity with the merest hint of a Welsh inflection.

M. Wynn Thomas, 'Prints of Wales: Contemporary Welsh Poetry in English', *Poetry in the British Isles* (University of Wales Press, 1995)

... people might think that writing poetry a strange thing to do. That is probably rather an un-Welsh attitude. With time that feeling has changed, helped by the fact that at least in Welsh language circles a poet is supposed to have a recognised role. He need not necessarily hide in academic life. The trouble with the idea of the community poet, the *bardd gwlad*, however, is that his writing seems to become a form of recreation. In the video world that's no bad thing, but personally I've always considered poetry a profession to which you're called, and I don't care if that sounds pretentious or not. Therefore, if I had been brought up elsewhere I think my opinion of what a poet is would have been different. Yet I've never wished to write in Welsh. Wales happens to be the place I find myself, and is at once typical and unique. A trip through any part of it would tell me this ...

Robert Minhinnick, from 'The Welsh Language and Anglo-Welsh Poets: a symposium' *Poetry Wales*, 20.1 (1984)

If you define literature in terms of language only, then a Welshman who writes in English is an English author — which should give Americans, Australians, Scotsmen and West Indians plenty to think about.

Gwyn Jones, *The Oxford Book of Welsh Verse in English* (OUP, 1977)

The true Wales is still to be found in the country. The heavy industries came from outside and are something new: but the country tradition runs back across the centuries as something essentially Welsh and every Welsh writer whatever his language has a responsibility in this respect.

R.S. Thomas, 'Anglo-Welsh Literature' in *R.S. Thomas: Selected Prose* ed. Sandra Anstey (Seren, 1995)

In a deracinated twentieth century, for whatever reason, Anglo-Welsh poets remain remarkably conscious of place .... 'Place' may refer to either a man-made or a natural world. Whereas the poetry of natural landscape has often been a feature of Anglo-Welsh literature, modern Wales is already post-industrial, and is as subject to the changes wrought by political decisions and scientific technology as anywhere else. An awareness that divisiveness and dereliction are an integral part of any description of the place has emerged powerfully in our contemporary poetry.

Jill Farringdon, 'Confessions of an Anglo-Welsh Reader', *New England Review and Bread Loaf Quarterly*, 1988

The younger Anglo-Welsh poets who, in contrast to the inclination of Anglo-Welsh poetry of the Sixties and Seventies to focus on 'traditional' Wales ... are extending their concern deep into urban and industrial areas of English-speaking Wales. This usually means, in fact, writing from where they are or where they come from, not only from their social circumstances but from their lives and their parents' lives. The result, according to some critics, is that they lose all specific Welshness.

... poets of the new movement are more tenacious of their present social reality, more inclined to defend or to wrestle with what they actually have, in places under great pressure or already partially devastated, and to resist the judgement of 'traditional' Welshness, as well as the condescension or indifference of English centralism.

Jeremy Hooker, 'Resistant Voices: Five Anglo-Welsh Poets', *Poetry Wales*, 22.3 (1987)

I am convinced that before a poet writing in English can fully justify his position as Anglo-Welsh, he needs either to write about

Welsh scenes, Welsh people, the Welsh past, life in contemporary Wales or his own analysis of all these or else to attempt to demonstrate in his verse those more elusive characteristics of style and feeling which are generally regarded as belonging to Welsh poetry.

Meic Stephens, 'The Second Flowering', *Poetry Wales*, 3.3 (1967)

Whether an English-language poem is Welsh or not is, I suggest, essentially a matter not of its verse-form or rhetoric, its physical setting or its cultural or political nationalism, but of its belonging to a body of work grounded in the experience of Wales as an entity with, as Trevor Fishlock has states it, "its own history, a different social and industrial development, special aspirations and problems." A *body* of work, by the single poet and his/her contemporaries — every poem need not testify to the writer's Welshness, any more than a black poet's every poem must express negritude, or a Christian poet's every poem must signify christening. What matters is particularity .... When a poet's work is grounded in the particularity that is Wales, then surely we have a Welsh poet.

Joseph Clancy, *Poetry Wales*, 20.4 (1985)

The poet who sets out to be consciously Welsh or to "permeate his work with those more elusive characteristics of style and feeling which are generally recognised as belonging to Welsh poetry" ... is not likely to write poetry. It seems mistaken to set our sights on a target minus a bullseye — the 'Welshness of Anglo-Welsh verse'; what we should be aiming at is the 'verseness' of the verse. The Welshness *is* and will be part of it but if you are only going to grub for that then you end up ... with a desperate provinicalism, a narrow literary nationalism.

Peter Gruffydd, 'Further to the Second Flowering', *Poetry Wales*, 4.1 (1968)

That a writer should recognise his own roots is a fine and enriching thing .... But no writer ought to be judged by the extent to which he does this. Nationalism can give a man a new strength of feeling, new ideas, an idealism, a fresh way of looking at the world around him. Other experiences are capable of doing the same, and I do not believe a writer ought to be given extra marks, as it were, for his commitment to a cause, or that he should repeat the old left-wing criticism of the Thirties, with Welsh nationalism substituted for Marxism.

Glyn Jones, *The Dragon Has Two Tongues* (Dent, 1968)

The creative urge does not march beneath a flag although it may from time to time astutely invoke its shade.

James Hamilton Paterson, *Gerontius* (Macmillan, 1989)

W.H. DAVIES
The Bed-sitting Room

Must I live here, with Scripture on my walls,
Death-cards with rocks and anchors; on my shelf
Plain men and women with plain histories
A proud landlady knows, and no one else?
Let me have pictures of a richer kind:
Scenes in low taverns, with their beggar rogues
Singing and drinking ale; who buy more joy
With a few pence than others can with pounds.
Show gypsies on wild commons, camped at fires
Close to their caravans; where they cook flesh
They have not bought, and plants not sold to them.
Show me the picture of a drinking monk
With his round belly like a mare in foal,
Belted, to keep his guts from falling out
When he laughs hearty; or a maid's bare back,
Who teases me with a bewitching smile
Thrown over her white shoulder. Let me see
The picture of a sleeping damosel,
Who has a stream of shining hair to fill
Up that deep channel banked by her white breasts.
Has Beauty never smiled from off these walls,
Has Genius never entered in a book?
Nay, Madam, keep your room; for in my box
I have a lovely picture of young Eve,
Before she knew what sewing was. Alas!
If I hung on your wall her naked form,
Among your graves and crosses, Scripture texts,
Your death-cards with their anchors and their rocks —
What then? I think this life a joyful thing,
And, like a bird that sees a sleeping cat,
I leave with haste your death-preparing room.

J is for Jealousy

I praised the daisies on my lawn,
And then my lady mowed them down.
My garden stones, improved by moss,
She moved — and that was Beauty's loss.
When I adored the sunlight, she

Kept a bright fire indoors for me.
She saw I loved the birds, and that
Made her one day bring home a cat.
She plucks my flowers to deck each room,
And make me follow where they bloom.
Because my friends were kind and many,
She said — 'What need has Love of any?'
What is my gain, and what my loss?
Fire without sun, stones bare of moss,
Daisies beheaded, one by one;
The birds cat-hunted, friends all gone —
These are my losses: yet, I swear,
A love less jealous in its care
Would not be worth the changing skin
That she and I are living in.

The Tugged Hand

I have no ears or eyes
    For either bird or flower;
Music and lovely blooms
    Must bide their lighter hour;
So let them wait awhile —
    For yet another day

Till I at last forget
    The woman lying dead;
And how a lonely child
    Came to his mother's bed
And tugged at her cold hand —
    And could not make it play.

EDWARD THOMAS
Women He Liked

Women he liked, did shovel-bearded Bob,
Old Farmer Hayward of the Heath, but he
Loved horses. He himself was like a cob,
And leather-coloured. Also he loved a tree.

For the life in them he loved most living things,
But a tree chiefly. All along the lane
He planted elms where now the stormcock sings
That travellers hear from the slow-climbing train.

Till then the track had never had a name
For all its thicket and the nightingales
That should have earned it. No one was to blame.
To name a thing beloved man sometimes fails.

Many years since, Bob Hayward died, and now
None passes there because the mist and the rain
Out of the elms have turned the lane to slough
And gloom, the name alone survives, Bob's Lane.

Celandine

Thinking of her had saddened me at first,
Until I saw the sun on the celandines lie
Redoubled, and she stood up like a flame,
A living thing, not what before I nursed,
The shadow I was growing to love almost,
The phantom, not the creature with bright eye
That I had thought never to see, once lost.

She found the celandines of February
Always before us all. Her nature and name
Were like those flowers, and now immediately
For a short swift eternity back she came,
Beautiful, happy, simply as when she wore
Her brightest bloom among the winter hues
Of all the world; and I was happy too,
Seeing the blossoms and the maiden who
Had seen them with me Februarys before,
Bending to them as in and out she trod
And laughed, with locks sweeping the mossy sod.

But this was a dream: the flowers were not true,
Until I stooped to pluck from the grass there
One of five petals and I smelt the juice
Which made me sigh, remembering she was no more,
Gone like a never perfectly recalled air.

Swedes

They have taken the gable from the roof of clay
On the long swede pile. They have let in the sun
To the white and gold and purple of curled fronds
Unsunned. It is a sight more tender-gorgeous
At the wood-corner where Winter moans and drips
Than when, in the Valley of the Tombs of Kings,
A boy crawls down into a Pharaoh's tomb
And, first of Christian men, beholds the mummy,
God and monkey, chariot and throne and vase,
Blue pottery, alabaster, and gold.

But dreamless long-dead Amen-hotep lies.
This is a dream of Winter, sweet as Spring.

Old Man

Old Man, or Lad's-love, — in the name there's nothing
To one that knows not Lad's-love, or Old Man,
The hoar-green feathery herb, almost a tree,
Growing with rosemary and lavender.
Even to one that knows it well, the names
Half decorate, half perplex, the thing it is:
At least, what that is clings not to the names
In spite of time. And yet I like the names.

The herb itself I like not, but for certain
I love it, as some day the child will love it
Who plucks a feather from the door-side bush
Whenever she goes in or out of the house.
Often she waits there, snipping the tips and shrivelling
The shreds at last on to the path, perhaps
Thinking, perhaps of nothing, till she sniffs
Her fingers and runs off. The bush is still
But half as tall as she, though it is as old;
So well she clips it. Not a word she says;
And I can only wonder how much hereafter
She will remember, with that bitter scent,
Of garden rows, and ancient damson trees
Topping a hedge, a bent path to a door,
A low thick bush beside the door, and me
Forbidding her to pick.

As for myself,
Where first I met the bitter scent is lost.
I, too, often shrivel the grey shreds,
Sniff them and think and sniff again and try
Once more to think what it is I am remembering,
Always in vain. I cannot like the scent,
Yet I would rather give up others more sweet,
With no meaning, than this bitter one.

I have mislaid the key. I sniff the spray
And think of nothing; I see and I hear nothing;
Yet seem, too, to be listening, lying in wait
For what I should, yet never can, remember:
No garden appears, no path, no hoar-green bush
Of Lad's-love, or Old Man, no child beside,
Neither father nor mother, nor any playmate;
Only an avenue, dark, nameless, without end.

And You, Helen

And you, Helen, what should I give you?
So many things I would give you
Had I an infinite great store
Offered me and I stood before
To choose. I would give you youth,
All kinds of loveliness and truth,
A clear eye as good as mine,
Lands, waters, flowers, wine,
As many children as your heart
Might wish for, a far better art
Than mine can be, all you have lost
Upon the travelling waters tossed,
Or given to me. If I could choose
Freely in that great treasure-house
Anything from any shelf,
I would give you back yourself,
And power to discriminate
What you want and want it not too late,
Many fair days free from care
And heart to enjoy both foul and fair,
And myself, too, if I could find
Where it lay hidden and it proved kind.

No One So Much As You

No one so much as you
Loves this my clay,
Or would lament as you
Its dying day.

You know me through and through
Though I have not told,
And though with what you know
You are not bold.

None ever was so fair
As I thought you:
Not a word can I bear
Spoken against you.

All that I ever did
For you seemed coarse
Compared with what I hid
Nor put in force.

My eyes scarce dare meet you
Lest they should prove
I but respond to you
And do not love.

We look and understand,
We cannot speak
Except in trifles and
Words the most weak.

For I at most accept
Your love, regretting
That is all: I have kept
Only a fretting

That I could not return
All that you gave
And could not ever burn
With the love you have,

Till sometimes it did seem
Better it were

Never to see you more
Than linger here

With only gratitude
Instead of love —
A pine in solitude
Cradling a dove.

A Private

This ploughman dead in battle slept out of doors
Many a frozen night, and merrily
Answered staid drinkers, good bedmen, and all bores:
'At Mrs Greenland's Hawthorn Bush', said he,
'I slept.' None knew which bush. Above the town,
Beyond 'The Drover', a hundred spot the down
In Wiltshire. And where now at last he sleeps
More sound in France — that, too, he secret keeps.

The Owl

Downhill I came, hungry, and yet not starved;
Cold, yet had heat within me that was proof
Against the North wind; tired, yet so that rest
Had seemed the sweetest thing under a roof.

Then at the inn I had food, fire, and rest,
Knowing how hungry, cold, and tired was I.
All of the night was quite barred out except
An owl's cry, a most melancholy cry

Shaken out long and clear upon the hill,
No merry note, nor cause of merriment,
But one telling me plain what I escaped
And others could not, that night, as in I went.

And salted was my food, and my repose,
Salted and sobered, too, by the bird's voice
Speaking for all who lay under the stars,
Soldiers and poor, unable to rejoice.

A.G. PRYS-JONES
The Wife of Carcassone

There was a man of Carcassone
Who put his buxom wife upon
A diet whereon lunch and dinner
Did not appear: so she grew thinner,
As thin, in fact, as any lath.
And one sad evening, in her bath
She slipped and slithered down the vent
Calling her husband as she went.
But he, alas, not understanding,
Stood wavering upon the landing,
Until a final gurgling noise
Disturbed his normal equipoise.
Then rushing round in fierce despair
He tried to find her everywhere.
He tapped the pipes, and then at once
Called down the sinks, without response:
He even dug the garden drain
And pushed the whole thing back again.
But nothing was the slightest use.

For she, now well adown the sluice
Beyond the clay-beds and the gravel
Without the vestige of apparel
But with an undulating motion,
Was heading swiftly for the ocean.
So nothing obvious could be done
For that poor wife of Carcassone.

Her husband, in strong sorrow pent,
Then knew he should have been content
To love her as the Lord had built her:
(Or fitted some safe bathroom filter
To meet the needs of her condition
As well he might, in his position.)

So now upon his lone veranda
He sits and muses on Miranda,
A charming wife whose tragic slimming
Was not offset by skill in swimming.

WILFRED OWEN
The Parable of the Old Man and the Young

So Abram rose, and clave the wood, and went,
And took the fire with him, and a knife.
And as they sojourned both of them together,
Isaac the first-born spake and said, My Father,
Behold the preparations, fire and iron,
But where the lamb for this burnt-offering?
Then Abram bound the youth with belts and straps,
And builded parapets and trenches there,
And stretchèd forth the knife to slay his son.
When lo! an angel called him out of heaven,
Saying, Lay not thy hand upon the lad,
Neither do anything to him. Behold,
A ram, caught in a thicket by its horns;
Offer the Ram of Pride instead of him.
But the old man would not so, but slew his son,
And half the seed of Europe, one by one.

The Send-off

Down the close, darkening lanes they sang their way
To the siding-shed,
And lined the train with faces grimly gay.

Their breasts were stuck all white with wreath and spray
As men's are, dead.

Dull porters watched them, and a casual tramp
Stood staring hard,
Sorry to miss them from the upland camp.
Then, unmoved, signals nodded, and a lamp
Winked to the guard.

So secretly, like wrongs hushed-up, they went.
They were not ours:
We never heard to which front these were sent.

Nor there if they yet mock what women meant
Who gave them flowers.

Shall they return to beatings of great bells
In wild train-loads?
A few, a few, too few for drums and yells,
May creep back, silent, to still village wells
Up half-known roads.

Dulce Et Decorum Est

Bent double, like old beggars under sacks,
Knock-kneed, coughing like hags, we cursed through
    sludge,
Till on the haunting flares we turned our backs
And towards our distant rest began to trudge.
Men marched asleep. Many had lost their boots
But limped on, blood-shod. All went lame; all blind;
Drunk with fatigue; deaf even to the hoots
Of tired, outstripped Five-Nines that dropped behind.

Gas! GAS! Quick, boys! — An ecstasy of fumbling,
Fitting the clumsy helmets just in time;
But someone still was yelling out and stumbling
And flound'ring like a man in fire or lime ...
Dim, through the misty panes and thick green light,
As under a green sea, I saw him drowning.

In all my dreams, before my helpless sight,
He plunges at me, guttering, choking, drowning.

If in some smothering dreams you too could pace
Behind the wagon that we flung him in,
And watch the white eyes writhing in his face,
His hanging face, like a devil's sick of sin;
If you could hear, at every jolt, the blood
Come gargling from the froth-corrupted lungs,
Obscene as cancer, bitter as the cud
Of vile, incurable sores on innocent tongues, —
My friend, you would not tell with such high zest
To children ardent for some desperate glory,
The old Lie: Dulce et decorum est
Pro patria mori.

Hospital Barge at Cérisy

Budging the sluggard ripples of the Somme,
A barge round old Cérisy slowly slewed.
Softly her engines down the current screwed
And chuckled in her, with contented hum,
Till fairy tinklings struck their crooning dumb,
And waters rumpling at the stern subdued.
The lock-gate took her bulging amplitude.
Gently into the gurgling lock she swum.

One, reading by that sunset raised his eyes
To watch her lessening westward quietly;
Till, as she neared the bend, her funnel screamed.
And that long lamentation made him wise
How unto Avalon in agony
Kings passed in the dark barge which Merlin dreamed.

Exposure

Our brains ache, in the merciless iced east winds that knive
    us ...
Wearied we keep awake because the night is silent ...
Low, drooping flares confuse our memory of the salient ...
Worried by silence, sentries whisper, curious, nervous,
        But nothing happens.

Watching, we hear the mad gusts tugging on the wire,
Like twitching agonies of men among its brambles.
Northward, incessantly, the flickering gunnery rumbles,
Far off, like a dull rumour of some other war.
        What are we doing here?

The poignant misery of dawn begins to grow ...
We only know war lasts, rain soaks, and clouds sag stormy.
Dawn massing in the east her melancholy army
Attacks once more in ranks on shivering ranks of gray,
        But nothing happens.

Sudden successive flights of bullets streak the silence.
Less deathly than the air that shudders black with snow,
With sidelong flowing flakes that flock, pause, and renew;

We watch them wandering up and down the wind's
    nonchalance,
        But nothing happens.

Pale flakes with fingering stealth come feeling for our faces —
We cringe in holes, back on forgotten dreams, and stare,
    snow-dazed,
Deep into grassier ditches. So we drowse, sun-dozed,
Littered with blossoms trickling where the blackbird fusses.
        Is it that we are dying?

Slowly our ghosts drag home: glimpsing the sunk fires,
    glozed
With crusted dark-red jewels; crickets jingle there;
For hours the innocent mice rejoice: the house is theirs;
Shutters and doors, all closed: on us the doors are closed, —
        We turn back to our dying.

Since we believe not otherwise can kind fires burn;
Nor ever suns smile true on child, or field, or fruit.
For God's invincible spring our love is made afraid;
Therefore, not loath, we lie out here; therefore were born,
        For love of God seems dying.

To-night, His frost will fasten on this mud and us,
Shrivelling many hands, puckering foreheads crisp.
The burying-party, picks and shovels in their shaking grasp,
Pause over half-known faces. All their eyes are ice,
        But nothing happens.

Futility

    Move him into the sun —
    Gently its touch awoke him once,
    At home, whispering of fields unsown.
    Always it woke him, even in France,
    Until this morning and this snow.
    If anything might rouse him now
    The kind old sun will know.

    Think how it wakes the seeds, —
    Woke, once, the clays of a cold star.

Are limbs, so dear-achieved, are sides,
Full-nerved — still warm — too hard to stir?
Was it for this the clay grew tall?
   — O what made fatuous sunbeams toil
To break earth's sleep at all?

Anthem for Doomed Youth

What passing-bells for these who die as cattle?
   Only the monstrous anger of the guns.
   Only the stuttering rifles' rapid rattle
Can patter out their hasty orisons.
No mockeries now for them; no prayers nor bells,
   Nor any voice of mourning save the choirs, —
The shrill, demented choirs of wailing shells;
   And bugles calling for them from sad shires.

What candles may be held to speed them all?
   Not in the hands of boys, but in their eyes
Shall shine the holy glimmers of good-byes.
   The pallor of girls' brows shall be their pall;
Their flowers the tenderness of patient minds,
And each slow dusk a drawing-down of blinds.

Strange Meeting

It seemed that out of battle I escaped
Down some profound dull tunnel, long since scooped
Through granites which titanic wars had groined.
Yet also there encumbered sleepers groaned,
Too fast in thought or death to be bestirred.
Then, as I probed them, one sprang up, and stared
With piteous recognition in fixed eyes,
Lifting distressful hands as if to bless.
And by his smile, I knew that sullen hall,
By his dead smile I knew we stood in Hell.
With a thousand pains that vision's face was grained;
Yet no blood reached there from the upper ground,
And no guns thumped, or down the flues made moan.
'Strange friend,' I said, 'here is no cause to mourn.'
'None,' said that other, 'save the undone years,

The hopelessness. Whatever hope is yours,
Was my life also; I went hunting wild
After the wildest beauty in the world,
Which lies not calm in eyes, or braided hair,
But mocks the steady running of the hour,
And if it grieves, grieves richlier than here.
For of my glee might many men have laughed,
And of my weeping something had been left,
Which must die now. I mean the truth untold,
The pity of war, the pity war distilled.
Now men will go content with what we spoiled,
Or, discontent, boil bloody, and be spilled.
They will be swift with swiftness of the tigress.
None will break ranks, though nations trek from progress.
Courage was mine, and I had mystery,
Wisdom was mine, and I had mastery:
To miss the march of this retreating world
Into vain citadels that are not walled.
Then, when much blood had clogged their chariot-wheels,
I would go up and wash them from sweet wells,
Even with truths that lie too deep for taint.
I would have poured my spirit without stint
But not through wounds; not on the cess of war.
Foreheads of men have bled where no wounds were.
I am the enemy you killed, my friend.
I knew you in this dark: for so you frowned
Yesterday through me as you jabbed and killed.
I parried; but my hands were loath and cold.
Let us sleep now ....'

DAVID JONES
from *In Parenthesis*
(Private John Ball wounded in the wood)

The trees are very high in the wan signal-beam, for whose slow gyration their wounded boughs seems as malignant limbs, manoeuvring for advantage.

    The trees of the wood beware each other
                    and under each a man sitting;
their seemly faces as carved in a sardonyx stone; as undiademed

princes turn their gracious profiles in a hidden seal, so did these appear, under the changing light.

For that waning you would believe this flaxen head had for its broken pedestal these bent Silurian shoulders.
 For the pale flares extinction you don't know if under his close lids, his eye-balls watch you. You would say by the turn of steel at his wide brow he is not of our men where he leans with his open fist in Dai's bosom against the White Stone.

Hung so about, you make between these your close escape.

The secret princes between the leaning trees have diadems given them.
 Life the leveller hugs her impudent equality — she may proceed at once to less discriminating zones.

The Queen of the Woods has cut bright boughs of various flowering.
 These knew her influential eyes. Her awarding hands can pluck for each their fragile prize.
 She speaks to them according to precedence. She knows what's due to this elect society. She can choose twelve gentle-men. She knows who is most lord between the high trees and on the open down.
 Some she gives white berries
                some she gives brown
 Emil has a curious crown it's
                made of golden saxifrage.
 Fatty wears sweet-briar,
he will reign with her for a thousand years.
 For Balder she reaches high to fetch his.
 Ulrich smiles for his myrtle wand.
 That swine Lilywhite has daisies to his chain — you'd hardly credit it.
 She plaits torques of equal splendour for Mr Jenkins and Billy Crower.
 Hansel with Gronwy share dog-violets for a palm, where they lie in serious embrace beneath the twisted tripod.
 Siôn gets St John's Wort — that's fair enough.
 Dai Great-coat, she can't find him anywhere — she calls both high and low, she had a very special one for him.

Among this July noblesse she is mindful of December wood —
when the trees of the forest beat against each other because of him.

She carries to Aneirin-in-the-nullah a rowan sprig, for the glory
of Guenedota. You couldn't hear what she said to him, because
she was careful for the Disciplines of the Wars.

At the gate of the wood you try a last adjustment, but slung so,
it's an impediment, it's of detriment to your hopes, you had best
be rid of it — the sagging webbing and all and what's left of your
two fifty — but it were wise to hold on to your mask.

You're clumsy in your feebleness, you implicate your tin-hat rim
with the slack sling of it.

Let it lie for the dews to rust it, or ought you to decently cover
the working parts.

Its dark barrel, where you leave it under the oak, reflects the
solemn star that rises urgently from Cliff Trench.

It's a beautiful doll for us
it's the Last Reputable Arm.

But leave it — under the oak.
Leave it for a Cook's tourist to the Devastated Areas and crawl as
far as you can and wait for the bearers.

Mrs Willy Hartington has learned to draw sheets and so has Miss
Melpomené; and on the south lawns,
men walk in red white and blue
under the cedars
and by every green tree
and beside comfortable waters.

But why dont the bastards come —
Bearers! — stret-cher bear-errs!

from *The Tribune's Visitation*

I have a word to say to you as men and as a man speaking to
men, but, and a necessary but, as a special sort of man speaking
to a special sort of men at a specific but recurring moment in
urbs-time.

Is this a hut on Apennine, where valley-gossips munch the chest-

nuts and croak Saturnian spells? Is this how guard-details stand
by for duties who guard the world-utilities?

Old rhyme, no doubt, makes beautiful
                         the older fantasies
but leave the stuff
                         to the men in skirts
who beat the bounds
                         of small localities
all that's done with
                         for the likes of us
in *Urbs*, throughout *orbis*.

It's not the brotherhood of the fields or the Lares of a remembered
hearth, or the consecrated wands bending in the fertile light to
transubstantiate for child-man the material vents and flows of
nature into the breasts and milk of the goddess.

                         Suchlike bumpkin sacraments
are for the young-time
                         for the dream-watches
now we serve contemporary fact.

                         It's the world-bounds
we're detailed to beat
                         to discipline the world-floor
to a common level
                         till everything presuming difference
and all the sweet remembered demarcations
                         wither
to the touch of us
                         and know the fact of empire.
Song? antique song
                         from known-site
spells remembered from the breast?
                         No!

But Latin song, you'll say, good song the fathers sang, the
aboriginal and variant alliterations known to each small *pagus*.

The remembered things of origin and streamhead, the things of the beginnings, of our own small beginnings.

                        The loved parts of that whole
which, when whole
                     subdued to wholeness
all the world.

These several streams, these local growths, all that belongs to the fields of Latium, to the Italic fatherland, surely these things, these dear pieties, should be remembered?

It stands to reason you'll say, these things, deep things, integral to ourselves, make for efficiency, steady the reg'mental will, make the better men, the better soldiers, so the better friends of Caesar.

                     No, not so
that pretty notion, too, must go.
                     Only the neurotic
look to their beginnings.

We are men of now and must strip as the facts of now would have it.

from *Tutelar of the Place*

Queen of the differentiated sites, administratrix of the demarcations, let our cry come unto you.
                     In all times of imperium save us when the *mercatores* come save us
                 from the guile of the *negotiatores* save us from the *missi*, from the agents
                     who think no shame
by inquest to audit what is shameful to tell
                        deliver us.
When they check their capitularies in their curias
                     confuse their reckonings.
When they narrowly assess the *trefydd*
                     by hide and rod

by *pentan* and pent
by impost and fee on beast-head
and roof-tree
and number the souls of men
notch their tallies false
disorder what they have collated.
When they proscribe the diverse uses and impose the
rootless uniformities, pray for us.
When they sit in *Consilium*
to liquidate the holy diversities
mother of particular perfections
queen of otherness
mistress of asymmetry
patroness of things counter, parti, pied, several
protectress of things known and handled
help of things familiar and small
wardress of the secret crevices
of things wrapped and hidden
mediatrix of all the deposits
margravine of the troia
empress of the labyrinth
receive our prayers.
When they escheat to the Ram
in the Ram's curia
the seisin where the naiad sings
above where the forked rod bends
or where the dark outcrop
tells on the hidden seam
pray for the green valley.

conclusion of *The Sleeping Lord*

Does he cock his weather-ear, enquiringly
lest what's on the west wind
from over beyond the rising contours
may signify that in the broken
tir y blaenau
these broken dregs of Troea
yet again muster?
Does he nudge his drowsing mate?
Do the pair of them
say to each other: 'Twere not other

than wind-cry, for sure — yet
        best to warn the serjeant below.
He'll maybe
        warn the Captain of the Watch
or some such
        and he, as like as not
may think best to rouse the Castellan
        — that'll please him
in his newly glazed, arras-hung chamber
        with his Dean-coal fire
nicely blazing
snug with his dowsabel
        in the inner keep
Wont improve his temper, neither, come the morrow
with this borough and hereabouts alerted
        and all for but a wind-bluster.
Still, you never know, so
        best stand on Standing Orders
and report to them as has the serjeancy
the ordering and mandate, for
you never know, mate:
        wind-stir may be, most like to be
as we between us do agree
        or — stir of gramarye
or whatsomever of ferly — who should say?
        or solid substantiality?
you never know *what* may be
        — not hereabouts.
No wiseman's son *born* do know
        not in these whoreson March-lands
of this Welshry.

Yet he sleeps on
        very deep is his slumber:
how long has he been the sleeping lord?
are the clammy ferns
        his rustling vallance
does the buried rowan
        ward him from evil, or
does he ward the tanglewood
        and the denizens of the wood
are the stunted oaks his gnarled guard

> or are their knarred limbs
strong with his sap?
Do the small black horses
> grass on the hunch of his shoulders?
are the hills his couch
> or is he the couchant hills?
Are the slumbering valleys
> him in slumber
> are the still undulations
the still limbs of him sleeping?
Is the configuration of the land
> the furrowed body of the lord
are the scarred ridges
> his dented greaves
do the trickling gullies
> yet drain his hog-wounds?
Does the land wait the sleeping lord
> or is the wasted land
that very lord who sleeps?

GWYN WILLIAMS
Wild Night at Treweithan

The evening's late November, clouds hump and streak,
the starlings are swept off-course in a black spray,
the gale howls and rattles in my wide chimney,
whistles in a nasty searching hurry.

The ponies can hardly believe it and face it
instead of turning their backsides as they usually do.
Is it drink makes me silly enough to think there's a force
that wants to get rid of something here before day?

The mountain's still black, the great chimneys
aren't rocked, the singing wires hold, we're
still linked to those others, I think of the farmhouse
as a hill-fort of stone with lines out over the moor.

No, there's no power to fear out there in the darkness,
only the idiot unpathed swirl of air belting
over this earth's face as we swing through hidden
stars. I have confidence in my grandfather's building.

Jet Planes

I've wished ill to the searing warplanes
that parallel my horizon and my hedgerows
I've learnt to estimate their line and cover
my ears for when they tear a furrow of thunder
between me and my neighbours' fields as they swoop
to our innocent almost bird-abandoned lake
and I've learnt not to curse them since
in cursing I harmed myself more than I harmed them
and their nasty games. I've thanked the mist
and the wild weather for grounding them but
now comes a change — today I thank them.
Thank you murderous faceless officials
who threw a shameless net of echoes
of sounds of war over our quiet region
for the net falls over the whole world binds me
to those who have been and will be killed
plucks me from my peaceable tenancy of earth
my selfish happiness to awareness of
those many-coloured millions like me
in the darkening continents of frightened man.

After Reading Poems to Einhir

I no longer wonder
who the yellow-haired girl was
who led Sorley Maclean
his agonised dance
through our stars
and politics.

I don't care who Dyddgu was
so long as Dafydd never
had her, nor that Beatrice
went to heaven before Dante
ever sniffed the nectar
of her body's odour,

Poor Tristan chaliced
unknowingly by Esyllt
and Myrddin mad changed

into the Merlin of Viviane's
Broceliande,
caught by the flesh.

But the golden girls and boys
who've sparked painful lust
in our discerning poets
are now to be thanked
for their cool turning away
from only burning hearts.

Fence in your charms
and farm them cleverly out
to safe bank-balanced lovers.
Deny the pleading poet.
Let's have his poems
and let your beauty rot.

IDRIS DAVIES
The Angry Summer 20

Look at the valleys down there in the darkness,
Long bracelets of twinkling lights,
And here with the mountain breeze on your brow
Consider the folk in the numberless streets
Between the long dark ridges, north to south.
Township after township lit up in long broken lines,
Silent and sparkling, sprinkling with jewels the night,
And Mrs Hughes and Mrs Rees rushing from shop to shop,
All fuss and bother, and Gwyneth and Blodwen
And slim young men hurrying now to the sixpenny dance,
And Shoni Bach Morris away to his pint,
And Ned and his wife and his kids in a crowd
Intent on the glamour of Hollywood;
Street intersecting street, and memorial clock in the circle,
The chemist's window radiant with cures for all complaints,
Lovers holding hands outside the furniture stores,
Bright buses sliding in from east and west,
And here's the toothless, barefoot old sailor at the corner

Yelling a song for your little brown penny.
London in little for one night in the week,
Red lights and green lights, and crowded pavements,
And who cares a damn on one night at least,
One night of tinsel, one night of jazz.
And one by one the lights shall go out
In all the valleys, leaving isolated lamps, silver pins,
Sticking into the inverted velvet of the midnight air.
And you shall listen then to the silence
That is not silence, to the murmur
Of the uneasy centuries among the ancient hills and valleys
As here you stand with the mountain breeze on your brow.

The Angry Summer 28

Hywel and Olwen are alone in the fern
On the hills behind the town,
Talking and kissing with lips that burn
As the sun of June goes down.

'O how can we marry, Olwen, my love,'
With me on a striker's pay?
How will you manage a home, my love,
Through the troubles of the day?'

'I will face all the troubles as others do,
Hywel my darling, my love,
And share in your battle through and through,
And live and die for love!'

Hywel and Olwen lie warm in the fern
With passionate mouth on mouth
And the lights in the valley twinkle and turn
And the moon climbs up from the south.

Gwalia Deserta VII

There are countless tons of rock above his head,
And gases wait in secret corners for a spark;
And his lamp shows dimly in the dust.
His leather belt is warm and moist with sweat,

And he crouches against the hanging coal,
And the pick swings to and fro,
And many beads of salty sweat play about his lips
And trickle down the blackened skin
To the hairy tangle on the chest.
The rats squeak and scamper among the unused props,
And the fungus waxes strong.

And Dai pauses and wipes his sticky brow,
And suddenly wonders if his baby
Shall grow up to crawl in the local Hell,
And if to-morrow's ticket will buy enough food for six days,
And for the Sabbath created for pulpits and bowler hats,
When the under-manager cleans a dirty tongue
And walks with the curate's maiden aunt to church ...

Again the pick resumes the swing of toil,
And Dai forgets the world where merchants walk in morning
　　streets,
And where the great sun smiles on pithead and pub and
　　church-steeple.

Gwalia Deserta XI

Dark gods of all our days,
　　Have mercy upon us.

Dark gods, take away
　　The shadows from our towns,

The hopeless streets, the hovels
　　Behind the colliery sidings.

Dark gods of grime and grief,
　　Soften the bitter day,

And give our children eyes
　　To see somewhere a summer.

Dark gods, we beg you,
　　Make us proud and angry,

That we shall rise from shame
    And imitate the torrent,

And scatter the high priests
    Who deal in blood and gold.

Dark gods of all our days,
    Dark gods of life and death,

Have mercy upon us
    Who wait in the shadow.

GLYN JONES
Again

Lamplight from our kitchen window-pane
Shines out on the leaves of the little apple-tree
Dripping in the rain.

Inside the warm room, those two women together
Cleaning the brass candlesticks in silence
Are my daughter and my mother.

She has become a woman to me, my daughter,
Her dress heavy with her breasts, her arms heavy;
She is desired now, she is a lover.

But what will have come to her, and been hers,
Her crooked hands idle on the table
And her feet slow on the stairs?

Her granny, tired out, her mouth dropped open,
Sits with her eyes shut, facing the lamplight.
She has seen so much happen.

Shall my daughter too run through the streets to the
    pit-head,
And stand cold among the women crowding the gateway,
And see the young men brought up dead?

Where All Were Good to Me, God Knows

Seeing the block of flats, I remember
The meadows under them, where Jones the Stoning's
Skewbald cart-horse would walk in sunshine
Camouflaged conspicuous as a tank,
Among the fluid swallows,
And the Jones's white-washed house,
And their long garden with the door in the wall,
In at which squat Russ and I floated and, through
Subaqueous gloom of their glass trees, out
On to their sunlit lawn, vast and glowing.

'Welcome, come in, my boy', said Mr Jones
— A shy man, he was never in the handshake
First to remit the pressure — adding
'zzz', when he saw there were two of us.
God bless much overfed, norfolk-suited,
Green-stockinged, yellow-booted Mr Jones
— Destined for his nest, must be, I thought, that fluff
Moustache — his high collar, his high colour
Glassy, tight over his shining head
The polished membrane of his tarry hair.

And his crippled Philip also, rowdiest
Hunchback goalie in the game — I remember
His brown hair-helmet (in sunlight the red
Gravy of sea-iron), his sad faces inked
On finger-nails, his nutmeg freckling,
The feel of crutch-pads warm from his armpits.

We played cards and ate apples,
While sweating Mr Jones, dumb talker,
Witty listener, sat watching us before
His red bed of flat sun-gulper tulips,
And the sun-soaked wall where deep udders
Of shadow hung down darkening the brickwork —
Beaming, his fat hand nursing his fat fist.

A raft of starlings exploded off the grass,
A full thrush hopped heavily with long
Kangaroo hops down the lawn and slowly
Mrs Jones followed, long-frocked from the dazzling house.
God bless his beautiful Mrs Jones also,

Her drake-head-green gown, her broad-brimmed hat,
    her cool
Face gold, radiant in lawn-reflected amber,
Her smile a mirror in which I smiled to see
Myself always clever, beautiful and good,
And before which off-white-handed Russ blushed
Into his shirt, and his aitches were the aitches,
Soon, of a boy who never sounded aitches.
    Mr Jones's face turned sharp out of shadow
Towards her, smiling, and some long curled tendril,
Some hot nostril hair, suddenly lit up red,
Glowed in sunlight like a burning filament.

All are dead, Jones the Stoning, Mrs Jones,
Philip, Russ, the charm, the tenderness, the glow.
Evening drops a vast sun into sunset
Where it smoulders swollen, boiling behind
The flats — once the great cart-horses pounded on
Pavings of those night-fall-slated meadows,
Where grey Danter, too, the Jones's pig-headed
Pony stood asleep beneath the burnt-out tree.
God bless beautiful flats also, I suppose.
Lights go on in windows. People live in them
And great stars flash among vanished branches
And night-owls call from elms no longer there.

The Seagull
(after Dafydd ap Gwilym)

Gracing the tide-warmth, this seagull,
The snow-semblanced, moon-matcher,
The sun-shard and sea-gauntlet
Floating, the immaculate loveliness.
The feathered one, fishfed, the swift-proud,
Is buoyant, breasting the combers.
Sea-lily, fly to this anchor to me,
Perch your webs on my hand.
You nun among ripples, habited
Brilliant as paper-work, come.
Girl-glorified you shall be, pandered to,

Gaining that castle mass, her fortalice.
Scout them out, seagull, those glowing battlements,
Reconnoitre her, the Eigr-complexioned.
Repeat my pleas, my citations, go
Girlward, gull, where I ache to be chosen.
She solus, pluck up courage, accost her,
Stress your finesse to the fastidious one;
Use honeyed diplomacy, hinting
I cannot remain extant without her.
I worship her, every particle worships!
Look, friends, not old Merddin, hot-hearted,
Not Taliesin the bright-browed, beheld
The superior of this one in loveliness.
Cypress-shapely, but derisive beneath
Her tangled crop of copper, gull,
O, when you eye all Christendom's
Loveliest cheek — this girl will bring
Annihilation upon me, should your answer
Sound, gull, no relenting note.

Dafydd's Seagull and the West Wind

Dafydd's Seagull Addresses Him

Sir, after all that sweet cod,
The soft soap and the maldod —
Moon-matcher, comber-lily,
Snow-semblanced nun of the sea! —
You made me, master, say yes,
And try to find her fortress.
But rather, since White-as-pith
Lived miles from Aberystwyth,
And you wanted an answer
In a flash, hot-hearted sir,
I passed on your passion's cry
*To the wind, my sub-*llatai,
My diving lover, my date,
My moth-soft-breathing playmate,
My perfume-picker, my tall
Tree-shudderer of crystal.

His Seagull Addresses The Wind

Wind, why could you not bring back
Some message for this maniac,
Some sign from that paragon
Up there beyond Pumlumon,
Some signal, relenting word?
Why leave his pleas unanswered?

Wind, my wings in ton-up dives
Buzzed on your barbs like beehives;
I felt on my taut midriff
And pinion-bones your soft biff,
As your back bronchoed the rings
Of my boisterous white buckings.
Contentious, and me a bridge,
Your reckless torrent — courage! —
Wrecked me, your blood-loud roarings
Crashed both arches of my wings.

Up sun-sloshed slopes your breath blows
A pilgrimage of shadows,
And, crowding above those stains,
White clouds, homers to mountains,
Their slow groping hands sightless,
You shepherd through the green press
Of peaks — you guide soft-fingered
Summit-fumblers, your blind herd.

Corn-ears clash, your brushing wings
Rouse their concerted peckings,
And sweep that albino sea
Black, the battling tall barley.

You, roaring forest-ghost, purr,
Roosting on boughs; your whisper,
In the jungle's throat, becomes
A rugger-roar of welcomes.
You sigh trees-full of pendant
Catkin-fringes in a slant,
Scattering sycamore keys
And ripe fire-blooms of poppies.

My wild wind, my gruff bellows,
Spoiler and boiler of boughs,
Why have you left me to face
Alone this mouth of menace?
Come, wind, from sodden mountains,
Drum down on him drenching rains,
Or else embrace his love-glow
Decked in your sea-coat of snow.

Fragment: Where is Tangwen now?

Where is Tangwen now, where Nest, where is Gwenllian,
    The apple-blossom and the summer's glow?
    Where are the 'gentle, gold-torqued maidens
Of this Island'? Where is Elen of the Hosts?
        Sun-bright Elen under her diadem,
        Gold and rubies and imperial stones?
    Mantled Elen in her milk-white silk, clasped
And girdled with red gold — yellow-haired Elen
    Of excelling beauty, on her golden throne,
    Her cheek upon her sleeping Emperor's cheek?
Where is Lleucu now, where Gwen, where golden
                Angharad?
Where are Betty Blythe and Vilma Banki and Laura La
                Plante?
        Where Eryl, the goddess — her stare,
Her hauteur, that we, her worshippers, believed could halt
        Chemistry at the confines of her body?
Where Rhiannon, enchantress, whose beauty crashed
                about our flesh,
    Blazing, golden as shattered nets of torn-down
Lightnings to catch us thunderstruck and staggered?
Slake me in moonshowers, cool Llio, crazy, I cried,
Wipe me in rainbows of your moon-mist loveliness.
    Where is Olwen, where Branwen, where Brengain?
Where Morfydd — her honeyed hair, her unshawled shoulders,
        Her marbled arms, beneath which nature,
            With accustomed insensitivity,
        Had placed a heavy tuft of low-grade hair?
Where is Pola Negri — Pola, the tingle of your teeth
        Like calvary, your lips like couches?

Where all the beautiful and high-class girls
Who let us finger them in the dark lanes of our village?
I have seen them since, tired in city supermarkets,
Thick-nosed, afflicted, grey, called Nana, buying
Cut-price toilet rolls in large quantities.
And lovely Mabli of the mental hospitals,
Mabli, dying alone in smelling sun, in the glass
Corridors of her mind's reclusion,
Grey-bearded, her lids down, silently
Wetting herself — and my voice brings back some
Tapping past upon her heart's abandoned panes,
And the anguished inmate, wild-eyed exile,
Rouses, croaking, 'Jesus Christ, the same
Yesterday, today, and for ever', — where
Is her lovely striding, her high laugh, her molten
Leopard-leap of wit and silken winds lifting
Her gold-red hair, sea-winds above her ears
Lifting that sunlight polished gold, word-
Drowning breeze between us on the sunlit beach —
And I awake again to hear, 'Jesus Christ, the same
Yesterday, today, and for ever', — and
I feel the shit-soaked feathers beat about my head,
The screeches wake me and the talons tear my heart.

VERNON WATKINS
The Collier

When I was born on Amman hill
A dark bird crossed the sun.
Sharp on the floor the shadow fell;
I was the youngest son.

And when I went to the County School
I worked in a shaft of light.
In the wood of the desk I cut my name:
Dai for Dynamite.

The tall black hills my brothers stood;
Their lessons all were done.

From the door of the school when I ran out
They frowned to watch me run.

The slow grey bells they rung a chime
Surly with grief or age.
Clever or clumsy, lad or lout,
All would look for a wage.

I learnt the valley flowers' names
And the rough bark knew my knees.
I brought home trout from the river
And spotted eggs from the trees.

A coloured coat I was given to wear
Where the lights of the rough land shone.
Still jealous of my favour
The tall black hills looked on.

They dipped my coat in the blood of a kid
And they cast me down in a pit,
And although I crossed with strangers
There was no way up from it.

Soon as I went from the County School
I worked in a shaft. Said Jim,
'You will get your chain of gold, my lad,
But not for a likely time.'

And one said, 'Jack was not raised up
When the wind blew out the light
Though he interpreted their dreams
And guessed their fears by night.'

And Tom, he shivered his leper's lamp
For the stain that round him grew;
And I heard mouths pray in the after-damp
When the picks would not break through.

They changed words there in darkness
And still through my head they run,
And white on my limbs is the linen sheet
And gold on my neck the sun.

The Heron

The cloud-backed heron will not move:
He stares into the stream.
He stands unfaltering while the gulls
And oyster-catchers scream.
He does not hear, he cannot see
The great white horses of the sea,
But fixes eyes on stillness
Below their flying team.

How long will he remain, how long
Have the grey woods been green?
The sky and the reflected sky,
Their glass he has not seen,
But silent as a speck of sand
Interpreting the sea and land,
His fall pulls down the fabric
Of all that windy scene.

Sailing with clouds and woods behind,
Pausing in leisured flight,
He stepped, alighting on a stone,
Dropped from the stars of night.
He stood there unconcerned with day,
Deaf to the tumult of the bay,
Watching a stone in water,
A fish's hidden light.

Sharp rocks drive back the breaking waves,
Confusing sea with air.
Bundles of spray blown mountain-high
Have left the shingle bare.
A shipwrecked anchor wedged by rocks,
Loosed by the thundering equinox,
Divides the herded waters,
The stallion and his mare.

Yet no distraction breaks the watch
Of that time-killing bird.
He stands unmoving on the stone;
Since dawn he has not stirred.
Calamity about him cries,

But he has fixed his golden eyes
On water's crooked tablet,
On light's reflected word.

Music of Colours — White Blossom

White blossom, white, white shell; the Nazarene
Walking in the ear; white touched by souls
Who know the music by which white is seen,
Blinding white, from strings and aureoles,
Until that is not white, seen at the two poles,
Nor white the Scythian hills, nor Marlowe's queen.

The spray looked white until this snowfall.
Now the foam is grey, the wave is dull.
Call nothing white again, we were deceived.
The flood of Noah dies, the rainbow is lived.
Yet from the deluge of illusions an unknown colour is saved.

White must die black, to be born white again
From the womb of sounds, the inscrutable grain,
From the crushed, dark fibre, breaking in pain.

The bud of the apple is already forming there.
The cherry-bud, too, is firm, and behind it the pear
Conspires with the racing cloud. I shall not look.
The rainbow is diving through the wide-open book
Past the rustling paper of birch, the sorceries of bark.

Buds in April, on the waiting branch,
Starrily opening, light raindrops drench,
Swinging from world to world when starlings sweep,
Where they alight in air, are white asleep.
They will not break, not break, until you say
White is not white again, nor may may.

White flowers die soonest, die into that chaste
Bride-bed of the moon, their lives laid waste.
Lilies of Solomon, taken by the gust,
Sigh, make way. And the dark forest
Haunts the lowly crib near Solomon's dust,
Rocked to the end of majesty, warmed by the low beast,
Locked in the liberty of his tremendous rest.

If there is white, or has been white, it must have been
When His eyes looked down and made the leper clean.
White will not be, apart, though the trees try
Spirals of blossom, their green conspiracy.
She who touched His garment saw no white tree.

Lovers speak of Venus, and the white doves,
Jubilant, the white girl, myth's whiteness, Jove's,
Of Leda, the swan, whitest of his loves.
Lust imagines him, web-footed Jupiter, great down
Of thundering light; love's yearning pulls him down
On the white swan-breast, the magical lawn,
Involved in plumage, mastered by the veins of dawn.

In the churchyard the yew is neither green nor black.
I know nothing of Earth or colour until I know I lack
Original white, by which the ravishing bird looks wan.
The mound of dust is nearer, white of mute dust that dies
In the soundfall's great light, the music in the eyes,
Transfiguring whiteness into shadows gone,
Utterly secret. I know you, black swan.

Ophelia

Stunned in the stone light, laid among the lilies,
Still in the green wave, graven in the reed-bed,
Lip-read by clouds in the language of the shallows,
Lie there, reflected.

Soft come the eddies, cold between your fingers.
Rippling through cresses, willow-trunk and reed-root,
Gropes the grey water; there the resting mayfly
Burns like an emerald.

Haunting the path, Laertes falls to Hamlet;
He, the young Dane, the mover of your mountains,
Sees the locked lids, your nunnery of sorrows,
Drowned in oblivion.

Silvered with dawn, the pattern of the bridge-vault
Dancing, a light-skein woven by the stream there,
Travels through shade the story of your dying,
Sweet-named Ophelia.

Dense was your last night, thick with stars unnumbered.
Bruised, the reeds parted. Under them the mud slipped,
Yielding. Scuttling and terrified, the moorhen
Left you to sink there.

Few, faint the petals carried on the surface,
Watched by those bright eyes ambushed under shadow,
Mouse, bird and insect, bore you witness, keeping
Pace ever silent.

Here, then, you lingered, late upon the world's rim,
Matched here the princelike, stopped, and were
    confounded,
Finding that image altered in the water's
Bitter remembrance.

Passion recalls the tumult of your story,
Midnight revives it, where your name is printed;
Yet from the water, intimate, there echoes:
'Tell this to no man'.

Bride-veils of mist fall, brilliant are the sunbeams,
Open the great leaves, all the birds are singing.
Still unawake in purity of darkness
Whiter than daylight

Dream the soft lids, the white, the deathly sleeping;
Closed are the lashes: day is there a legend.
Rise from the fair flesh, from the midnight water,
Child too soon buried.

LYNETTE ROBERTS
Poem from Llanybri

If you come my way that is ...
Between now and then, I will offer you
A fist full of rock cress fresh from the bank
The valley tips of garlic red with dew
Cooler than shallots, a breath you can swank

In the village when you come. At noon-day
I will offer you a choice bowl of cawl
Served with a 'lover's' spoon and a chopped spray
Of leeks or savori fach, not used now

In the old way you'll understand. The din
Of children singing through the eyelet sheds
Ringing 'smith hoops, chasing the butt of hens;
Or I can offer you Cwmcelyn spread

With quartz stones, from the wild scratchings of men;
You will have to go carefully with clogs
Or thick shoes for it's treacherous the fen,
The East and West Marshes also have bogs.

Then I'll do the lights, fill the lamp with oil,
Get coal from the shed, water from the well;
Pluck and draw pigeon with crop of green foil
This your good supper from the lime-tree fell.

A sit by the hearth with blue flames rising,
No talk. Just a stare at 'Time' gathering
Healed thoughts, pool insight, like swan sailing
Peace and sound around the home, offering

You a night's rest and my day's energy.
You must come, start this pilgrimage,
Can you come? — send an ode or elegy
In the old way and raise our heritage.

JEAN EARLE
Visiting Light

A single rose-red tile
On an opposite roof
Comes and goes among adjacent slates,
According to light, weather.
Rain, blown off the spring river,
Brings it up proud
Of surrounding greys —
Like an expected face, flushing.

Roofs fascinate —
How they straddle families,
Equal across the too-many
As over the so-lonely,
Giving nothing away.
Discreet above violent stoves,
Cold or much-tumbled beds —
The small saucepan with one furtive egg,
All he can or all he will
Allow himself — which?

Here broods a latent poetry
Nobody reads.
The weed that has managed flowers,
Pinched in a crack,
Lays its thin shadow down
In the afternoons; as a new mother will,
In the room below.

Jackdaws are in these chimneys,
Their difficult lives
Reflect our own; but who will be awake
For the luminous dawn
When the young fly for the first time?

Jackdaws seem inimical
To the mosses, disrupt them down
To me, as I clean my step,
Rubbing with bluestone in the old way.
My scour against the world's indifference
To important symbols — the common roof,
Likeness of patterns.
How warm this moss is,
In my cross hand! A minuscule forest
Full of see-through deaths
That should have had wings ....

'Under one roof'
Is such an old expression,
Steady and parental —
Yet life beneath,
Hidden by the roof, changes pace

Daring and malicious as jackdaws,
Unpredictable
As visiting light: or the one rose-red tile
Flushing up — vanishing.

Jugged Hare

She mourned the long-ears
Hung in the pantry, his shot fur
Softly dishevelled. She smoothed that,
Before gutting — yet she would rather
Sicken herself, than cheat my father
Of his jugged hare.

A tender lady, freakish as the creature —
But resolute. She peeled it to its tail.
Oh, fortitude! Her rings sparked in and out
Of newspaper wipes. Blood in a bowl,
Sacrificial gravy. A rarely afforded
Bottle of port.

She sustained marriage
On high events, as a child plays house.
Dramas, conciliations —
Today, the hare. She sent me out
To bury the skin,
Tossed the heart to the cat.

She was in full spate.

Fragrance of wine and herbs
Blessed our kitchen; like the hare's dessert
Of wild thyme; or like his thighs
As though braised by God. She smiled
And dished up on willow,
Having a nice touch in framing
One-off scenarios.

After the feast, my father was a lover
Deeply enhanced.
I heard them go to bed,
Kissing — still inside her picture.

Later, I heard her sob
And guessed it was the hare
Troubled her. My father slept,
Stunned with tribute. She lay now
Outside her frame, in the hare's dark

Hating her marital skills
And her lady-hands, that could flense a hare
Because she wooed a man.
In years to come,
I understood.

Old Tips

Over the years, a tip would take on time's finish,
A greening over —
Seen from far off, a patina
As on bronze memorials. It was a feature
Of place and weather, one of the marks of home
To my springloaded people.

Autumn in the allotments; sunlit on high,
The town shadowed. All the pits asleep.
Sometimes, cows off a neglected farm
Would stray across a very old tip —
Lie around on the strange, wispy grass,
Comforting their udders.
Old tips breathed out a warm, greenish smoke
After rain,
Suggesting thin, volcanic pastures.

Some tips were famed as wicked, secreting runnels
Of dark, treacle death; swallowing houses
Helpless at their feet.
But most were friendly —
We children ran out of school
Visiting the one that rose
Close to our playground.
We scrambled towards the top —
To shriek the dandelion flaring in the grit
And that abandoned crane,
Pointing to the annual sea.

Blondie

Most days, this wild weather,
Our bus picks up a girl
Whose splendid hair lights up the rattling box,
Trespasses, undrawn,
Over the back of her seat.

Ideal beauty — Helen's or Isolde's —
How can we be sure
These timeless ladies' lure
Was blonde and beautiful?
Because the torch of it lives on
In everyman's blood,
Continuing fire.

I have seen a man,
Sitting behind, advance trembling fingers,
Seemingly unaware
Of his mesmerised touch

As when the monks dug up
Arthur and Guinevere, that queen
Lay with her great yellow plaits unfaded —
So their fascinated hands
Must have presumed.

She comes to her stop,
Hurries the shining mane
Cometwise through the bus. Thuds down.
Wind and rain ravel the gold across
Her pudding face.

Backgrounds Observed

Peering, in depth,
Behind the lovers, murderers,
Intriguing corpses —
To lamps, ornaments,
Even a cushion like one of ours,
Backfill windows
Rushed with Hollywood rain ....

Are these things meaningful
To the enacted scene? And, if so,
Why seldom noticed?

Is it to do with differences
Between truth and fiction?
Rose gardens, panelled rooms,
Enhance Jane Austen serials
Like a bodice trim, taken for granted —
Yet documentaries
Advance their settings, as binoculars
Feather a nest.

Therefore, surprised, behind Kim Philby's shoulder
We spy that cabinet
Of fine china. And one of the 'boys'
(So-called) who created the Bomb ...
Svelte as they come, with a lovable grin ...
Fronting a hedge we might not note
But for the contrast
With his terrible presence. Such delicate blossom!

The Tea Party

I asked my dead to tea.
Accumulated news pointed my tongue
Like a pin through silks, like a crammed bee-bag,
Heavy to unload.

They sat in the garden,
Smiling the stone-burnt roll-call of their names.
I set a table between roses,
Laid with their favourite things.

Oh, my sweet dead — the cakes, the cakes!
All news discharged to the faint, receptive sheen
Of your listening eyes. Then, for the first time
I knew that you were dead at last, and I —

Healed?

It came upon me with the emptied teapot
And the westering sun. I had no plans for you
Beyond the afternoon.

Exits

Seep yourself, clear as water,
Into the vase
Of some other form — any shape you please.
Breakherb to turn all keys
Is in the mind's box.

From a lifetime of looking, the art perfects
Suddenly. It comes best
When one is old: as when, through open house,
I glimpsed a ray on a picture
I had known forever.
I knew it was of the sea. Ray and distance
Eclipsed it; yet all at once,
I was in it. I heard the gull,
Rode on the wave
Sweeping to break — that for years had been
Static to the wall.

If you have loved the world enough,
You can make escapes
Into any thing; and need not stay
Beyond strength, work to be done
Or those who watch (as for bad news)
Your timeless absences.

Look — hard — and go. Hovering, moving in
To your relief. There is no transcendence
Like this changeover.

How is it with you then, ventured inside
Another entity?

Refreshed.

If you should find yourself so poor
No tempting exits offer —

Try slipping your mood
Into a freeze, or a thaw. A stone, even ....
Always a stone; but set sometimes with sly
Sparkle. A little death,
For as long or as brief acquaintance
As you choose.

Note: Breakherb: a magic herb that opens locks.

The May Tree

Now they are old, on dull mornings —
Nothing to get up for —
Wrinkles hardly show
Behind drawn curtains.
Under the side lamp
White hair sheens gold.

After early tea, while they keep warm
Under the duvet,
Something comes over them and they make love,
Much as when young ....
Easing each other, without care
What 'anyone' might think
If 'anyone' knew. Why not?

Eyes without glasses see the world
Not as it is but as it was.
They find redundant, soft
Still-wild places. Their old age
Is bold as brass.

She recovers first; as women do.
He naps on.

Like a knock at the door
Comes a may tree she has
Sometimes remembered. How it went mad
With scent and snow, spending itself
On to the earth; yet there was more and more
Celebration, long after time to stop.

Next year, it died.

She looks at this; and stamps on the connection,
Manfully; as women do.

BRENDA CHAMBERLAIN
Seal Cave

Far down, in the pool below me,
At the base of yellow rock walls,
A monster barks.
It is the bull seal,
Blowing, threshing and flowing,
Nine feet of smooth-packed flesh.
Green as oil, he comes
Out of the secret cavern,
The mammalian bedroom,
Into open water's emerald waves,
And is aware, through their invincible
Rise and fall
Of how I admire his performance.
Though he turns an aquiline profile
And hoods his eyes with heavy lids,
He is nonetheless aware.

From the pulsating
Jewel-coloured sea, from white foam-lace,
Rises a gentle stone-grey head, whiskered, soft-eyed.
Dappled, white-breasted, vulnerable,
Gleaming like a fish, it is a cow of his harem.
Hola, hola, hola, seal cow!
She dives down the entrance tunnel, into the pool;
Her mottled back, where it touches the surface
Becoming iridescent as mother-of-pearl.
Those brown beseeching eyes would have me go to her,
Would drag me down.
Those almost human hands extended,
Then folded inwards to the breast,
Say come, come, come,
To caverns where whale-bones lie

Bleached and growth-ringed.
Mother seal, seal cow,
Your eyes almost compel me to a salt death.
Your eyes are so full of knowledge,
It would be no surprise
To find you had understanding
Of how it is I am a lonely woman
Living on a lonely strand:
Of how it is, that when in the Spring I am crowned,
It is but with sea-tangle and shells.

Evening has come. It is cold on this sunless rock
Past which waves hurry in tumult.
The moon rises in the wind-whipped sky
Over the flood pouring relentlessly past.
The sea is cold: the moon is cold.
O virginal Spring moon!

HENRY TREECE
Conquerors

By sundown we came to a hidden village
Where all the air was still
And no sound met our tired ears, save
For the sorry drip of rain from blackened trees
And the melancholy song of swinging gates.
Then through a broken pane some of us saw
A dead bird in a rusting cage, still
Pressing his thin tattered breast against the bars,
His beak wide open. And
As we hurried through the weed-grown street,
A gaunt dog started up from some dark place
And shambled off on legs as thin as sticks
Into the wood, to die at least in peace.
No-one had told us victory was like this;
Not one amongst us would have eaten bread
Before he'd filled the mouth of the grey child
That sprawled, stiff as a stone, before the shattered door.
There was not one who did not think of home.

Y Ddraig Goch

The dragon of our dreams roared in the hills
That ring the sunlit land of children's songs.
Red with the lacquer of a fairy-tale,
His fiery breath fried all besieging knights.
Whole seasons could he lay the land in waste
By puffing once upon the standing corn!

He was our dragon dressed in red, who kept
Sly ghosts from lurking underneath the thatch,
And made the hen lay dark-brown eggs for tea.
One word to him, just as you went to bed,
Made Twm, the postman, call next afternoon;
'Ho, bachgen,' that is what he'd say, 'Just look,
A fine blue postal-order from your Mam!
Twm gets a pint for bring that, I bet!'

The dragon cured us when the measles came,
And let the mare drop me a coal-black foal.
He taught us where nests lay, and found us fish,
Then thawed the snow to save the winter lamb.

Ho, Ddraig Goch, my pretty, pretty friend!
We were his children, knowing all his ways;
We laid out nightly gifts beneath the hedge,
Five linnet's eggs, a cup, a broken whip,
And heard his gracious sighs sweep through the trees.
But tears for all the fools who called him false!
One lad who sniggered fell down Parry's well;
The English Parson had a plague of warts;
Old Mrs Hughes was bitten by a cat;
The school roof fell in when the teacher smiled!

Ho, Ddraig Goch, they tell me you are dead;
They say they heard you weeping in the hills
For all your children gone to London Town.
They say your tears set Tawe in a flood.
I'm older now, but still I like to think
Of your great glass-green eyes fixed on the Fferm,
Guarding the children, keeping them from harm.

Don't die, old dragon, wait a few years more,
I shall come back and bring you boys to love.

MICHAEL BURN
Welsh Love Letter

Were all the peaks of Gwynedd
In one huge mountain piled,
Cnicht on Moelwyn,
Moel-y-gest, Moel Hebog,
And Eryri on top,
And all between us,
I'd climb them climb them
All!
To reach you.
O, how I love you!

Were all the streams of Gwynedd
In one great river joined,
Dwyfor, Dwyryd,
Glaslyn, Ogwen,
And Mawddach in flood,
And all between us,
I'd swim them swim them
All!
To reach you.
O, how I love you!

Were all the forts of Gwynedd
In one great fortress linked,
Caer and castle,
Criccieth, Harlech,
Conwy, Caernarfon,
And all in flames,
I'd jump them jump them
All!
To reach you.
O, how I love you!

See you Saturday,
If it's not raining.

In Japan

In Japan the poets write to each other:
'I wish I could write like you.
I go on dabbing at screens with my tired brushwork.
Yours is so brave and new.'

In Japan the poets reply to each other:
'The first polish of words is mine
Which produces a mist. The second (Esteemed Sir)
Is yours, which makes them shine.'

In Japan the poets cable the critics:
'Disgusted at line you took
About my latest stop how dare honoured sir
Recommend so worthless book.'

In Japan the poets write to the editors:
'Thanks for returning enclosure
To this insignificant person, thereby
Saving him public exposure.'

In Japan the poets say to the public:
'Thank you for being immense.
I refund in part for poems that have no rhythm.
In full if they have no sense.'

And publishers receive verses
In paint on a feathered fan:
'This humble singer rejoices in those you left out.'
That's how it is in Japan.

R.S. THOMAS
Welsh Landscape

To live in Wales is to be conscious
At dusk of the spilled blood
That went to the making of the wild sky,
Dyeing the immaculate rivers
In all their courses.
It is to be aware,

Above the noisy tractor
And hum of the machine
Of strife in the strung woods,
Vibrant with sped arrows.
You cannot live in the present,
At least not in Wales.
There is the language for instance,
The soft consonants
Strange to the ear.
There are cries in the dark at night
As owls answer the moon,
And thick ambush of shadows,
Hushed at the fields' corners.
There is no present in Wales,
And no future;
There is only the past,
Brittle with relics,
Wind-bitten towers and castles
With sham ghosts;
Mouldering quarries and mines;
And an impotent people,
Sick with inbreeding,
Worrying the carcase of an old song.

Cynddylan on a Tractor

Ah, you should see Cynddylan on a tractor.
Gone the old look that yoked him to the soil;
He's a new man now, part of the machine,
His nerves of metal and his blood oil.
The clutch curses, but the gears obey
His least bidding, and lo, he's away
Out of the farmyard, scattering hens.
Riding to work now as a great man should,
He is the knight at arms breaking the fields'
Mirror of silence, emptying the wood
Of foxes and squirrels and bright jays.
The sun comes over the tall trees
Kindling all the hedges, but not for him
Who runs his engine on a different fuel.
And all the birds are singing, bills wide in vain,
As Cynddylan passes proudly up the lane.

A Welsh Testament

All right, I was Welsh. Does it matter?
I spoke the tongue that was passed on
To me in the place I happened to be,
A place huddled between grey walls
Of cloud for at least half the year.
My word for heaven was not yours.
The word for hell had a sharp edge
Put on it by the hand of the wind
Honing, honing with a shrill sound
Day and night. Nothing that Glyn Dŵr
Knew was armour against the rain's
Missiles. What was descent from him?

Even God had a Welsh name:
We spoke to him in the old language;
He was to have a peculiar care
For the Welsh people. History showed us
He was too big to be nailed to the wall
Of a stone chapel, yet still we crammed him
Between the boards of a black book.

Yet men sought us despite this.
My high cheek-bones, my length of skull
Drew them as to a rare portrait
By a dead master. I saw them stare
From their long cars, as I passed knee-deep
In ewes and wethers. I saw them stand
By the thorn hedges, watching me string
The far flocks on a shrill whistle.
And always there was their eyes' strong
Pressure on me: You are Welsh, they said;
Speak to us so; keep your fields free
Of the smell of petrol, the loud roar
Of hot tractors; we must have peace
And quietness.

                Is a museum
Peace? I asked. Am I the keeper
Of the heart's relics, blowing the dust
In my own eyes? I am a man;
I never wanted the drab rôle
Life assigned me, an actor playing

To the past's audience upon a stage
Of earth and stone; the absurd label
Of birth, of race hanging askew
About my shoulders. I was in prison
Until you came; your voice was a key
Turning in the enormous lock
Of hopelessness. Did the door open
To let me out or yourselves in?

On the Farm

There was Dai Puw. He was no good.
They put him in the fields to dock swedes,
And took the knife from him, when he came home
At late evening with a grin
Like the slash of a knife on his face.

There was Llew Puw, and he was no good.
Every evening after the ploughing
With the big tractor he would sit in his chair,
And stare into the tangled fire garden,
Opening his slow lips like a snail.

There was Huw Puw, too. What shall I say?
I have heard him whistling in the hedges
On and on, as though winter
Would never again leave those fields,
And all the trees were deformed.

And lastly there was the girl:
Beauty under some spell of the beast.
Her pale face was the lantern
By which they read in life's dark book
The shrill sentence: God is love.

The Bright Field

I have seen the sun break through
to illuminate a small field
for a while, and gone my way
and forgotten it. But that was the pearl
of great price, the one field that had
the treasure in it. I realize now

that I must give all that I have
to possess it. Life is not hurrying

on to a receding future, nor hankering after
an imagined past. It is the turning
aside like Moses to the miracle
of the lit bush, to a brightness
that seemed as transitory as your youth
once, but is the eternity that awaits you.

Geriatric

What god is proud
        of this garden
of dead flowers, this underwater
        grotto of humanity,
where limbs wave in invisible
        currents, faces drooping
on dry stalks, voices clawing
        in a last desperate effort
to retain hold? Despite withered
        petals, I recognise
the species: Charcot, Ménière,
        Alzheimer. There are no gardeners
here, caretakers only
        of reason overgrown
by confusion. This body once,
        when it was in bud,
opened to love's kisses. These eyes,
        cloudy with rheum,
were clear pebbles that love's rivulet
        hurried over. Is this
the best Rabbi Ben Ezra
        promised? I come away
comforting myself, as I can,
        that there is another
garden, all dew and fragrance,
        and that these are the brambles
about it we are caught in,
        a sacrifice prepared
by a torn god to a love fiercer
        than we can understand.

A Marriage

We met
      under a shower
of bird-notes.
      Fifty years passed,
love's moment
      in a world in
servitude to time.
      She was young;
I kissed with my eyes
      closed and opened
them on her wrinkles.
      'Come,' said death,
choosing her as his
      partner for
the last dance. And she,
      who in life
had done everything
      with a bird's grace,
opened her bill now
      for the shedding
of one sigh no
      heavier than a feather.

Still

You waited with impatience
each year for the autumn migration.
It happened and was over.

Your turn then. You departed,
not southward into the burnished
and sunlit country, but out

into the dark, where there are
no poles, no accommodating
horizons. Last night, as I loitered

where your small bones had their nest,
the owl blew away from your stone cross
softly as down from a thistle-head. I wondered.

CLIFFORD DYMENT
'As a Boy With a Richness of Needs I Wandered'

As a boy with a richness of needs I wandered
In car parks and streets, epicure of Lagondas,
Minervas, Invictas, and Hispano Suizas;
And I sampled as roughage and amusing sauce
Rovers and Rileys, and the occasional funny
Trojan with chain drive, and the Morris Cowleys
With their modest bonnets, sedate Fiat
Of the nineteen-twenties, and the Alvis, middle-brow
Between the raffish sports car and the family bus.
I was tempted by aircraft, too, sniffing
Over *The Aeroplane* and *Flight* — those kites,
They seem today, knocked up in a backyard
By young and oily artists who painted with rivets:
Westland Wapiti, Bristol Bulldog and the great
De Havilland Hercules, invading the desert
And pulsing within its sleep like a troubling nerve;
And surely, I think, as I remember those feasts,
They were days of excitement and lavish surprise?
Where is the tantalizing richness and hazard
Of assertive styling, of crazy rigs,
Now that a car is unremarkably one of a million,
And an aeroplane a tubular schedule? I wander
Still in the car parks, but now uneasily,
Thinking that engineering is a sort of evolution —
Out of the fittest come the many merely fit;
And I wonder if I am wrong, or the world, whose aspect
Is nowhere strange, but is nowhere home.

The Swans

Midstream they met. Challenger and champion,
They fought a war for honour
Fierce, sharp, but with no honour:
Each had a simple aim and sought it quickly.
The combat over, the victor sailed away
Broken, but placid as is the gift of swans,
Leaving his rival to his shame alone.
I listened for a song, according to story,
But this swan's death was out of character —

No giving up of the grace of life
In a sad lingering music.
I saw the beaten swan rise on the water
As though to outreach pain, its webbed feet
Banging the river helplessly, its wings
Loose in a last hysteria. Then the neck
Was floating like a rope and the swan was dead.
It drifted away and all around it swan's-down
Bobbed on the river like children's little boats.

DYLAN THOMAS
'The Hand That Signed the Paper Felled a City'

The hand that signed the paper felled a city;
Five sovereign fingers taxed the breath,
Doubled the globe of dead and halved a country;
These five kings did a king to death.

The mighty hand leads to a sloping shoulder,
The finger joints are cramped with chalk;
A goose's quill has put an end to murder
That put an end to talk.

The hand that signed the treaty bred a fever,
And famine grew, and locusts came;
Great is the hand that holds dominion over
Man by a scribbled name.

The five kings count the dead but do not soften
The crusted wound nor pat the brow;
A hand rules pity as a hand rules heaven;
Hands have no tears to flow.

After the Funeral
(in memory of Ann Jones)

After the funeral, mule praises, brays,
Windshake of sailshaped ears, muffle-toed tap
Tap happily of one peg in the thick
Grave's foot, blinds down the lids, the teeth in black,
The spittled eyes, the salt ponds in the sleeves,

Morning smack of the spade that wakes up sleep,
Shakes a desolate boy who slits his throat
In the dark of the coffin and sheds dry leaves,
That breaks one bone to light with a judgment clout,
After the feast of tear-stuffed time and thistles
In a room with a stuffed fox and a stale fern,
I stand, for this memorial's sake, alone
In the snivelling hours with dead, humped Ann
Whose hooded, fountain heart once fell in puddles
Round the parched worlds of Wales and drowned each sun
(Though this for her is a monstrous image blindly
Magnified out of praise; her death was a still drop;
She would not have me sinking in the holy
Flood of her heart's fame; she would lie dumb and deep
And need no druid of her broken body).
But I, Ann's bard on a raised hearth, call all
The seas to service that her wood-tongued virtue
Babble like a bellbuoy over the hymning heads,
Bow down the walls of the ferned and foxy woods
That her love sing and swing through a brown chapel,
Bless her bent spirit with four, crossing birds.
Her flesh was meek as milk, but this skyward statue
With the wild breast and blessed and giant skull
Is carved from her in a room with a wet window
In a fiercely mourning house in a crooked year.
I know her scrubbed and sour humble hands
Lie with religion in their cramp, her threadbare
Whisper in a damp word, her wits drilled hollow,
Her fist of a face died clenched on a round pain;
And sculptured Ann is seventy years of stone.
These cloud-sopped, marble hands, this monumental
Argument of the hewn voice, gesture and psalm,
Storm me forever over her grave until
The stuffed lung of the fox twitch and cry Love
And the strutting fern lay seeds on the black sill.

Poem in October

It was my thirtieth year to heaven
Woke to my hearing from harbour and neighbour wood
And the mussel pooled and the heron
Priested shore

The morning beckon
With water praying and call of seagull and rook
And the knock of sailing boats on the net webbed wall
          Myself to set foot
               That second
     In the still sleeping town and set forth.

     My birthday began with the water-
Birds and the birds of the winged trees flying my name
     Above the farms and the white horses
               And I rose
               In rainy autumn
And walked abroad in a shower of all my days.
High tide and the heron dived when I took the road
          Over the border
               And the gates
     Of the town closed as the town awoke.

     A springful of larks in a rolling
Cloud and the roadside bushes brimming with whistling
     Blackbirds and the sun of October
               Summery
          On the hill's shoulder,
Here were fond climates and sweet singers suddenly
Come in the morning where I wandered and listened
          To the rain wringing
               Wind blow cold
     In the wood faraway under me.

     Pale rain over the dwindling harbour
And over the sea wet church the size of a snail
     With its horns through mist and the cattle
               Brown as owls
          But all the gardens
Of spring and summer were blooming in the tall tales
Beyond the border and under the lark full cloud.
          There could I marvel
               My birthday
     Away but the weather turned around.

     It turned away from the blithe country
And down the other air and the blue altered sky
     Streamed again a wonder of summer

With apples
Pears and red currants
And I saw in the turning so clearly a child's
Forgotten mornings when he walked with his mother
Through the parables
Of sun light
And the legends of the green chapels

And the twice told fields of infancy
That his tears burned my cheeks and his heart moved in mine.
These were the woods the river and sea
Where a boy
In the listening
Summertime of the dead whispered the truth of his joy
To the trees and the stones and the fish in the tide.
And the mystery
Sang alive
Still in the water and singingbirds.

And there could I marvel my birthday
Away but the weather turned around. And the true
Joy of the long dead child sang burning
In the sun.
It was my thirtieth
Year to heaven stood there then in the summer noon
Though the town below lay leaved with October blood.
O may my heart's truth
Still be sung
On this high hill in a year's turning.

The Hunchback in the Park

The hunchback in the park
A solitary mister
Propped between trees and water
From the opening of the garden lock
That lets the trees and water enter
Until the Sunday sombre bell at dark

Eating bread from a newspaper
Drinking water from the chained cup
That the children filled with gravel

In the fountain basin where I sailed my ship
Slept at night in a dog kennel
But nobody chained him up.

Like the park birds he came early
Like the water he sat down
And Mister they called Hey mister
The truant boys from the town
Running when he had heard them clearly
On out of sound

Past lake and rockery
Laughing when he shook his paper
Hunchbacked in mockery
Through the loud zoo of the willow groves
Dodging the park keeper
With his stick that picked up leaves.

And the old dog sleeper
Alone between nurses and swans
While the boys among willows
Made the tigers jump out of their eyes
To roar on the rockery stones
And the groves were blue with sailors

Made all day until bell time
A woman figure without fault
Straight as a young elm
Straight and tall from his crooked bones
That she might stand in the night
After the locks and chains

All night in the unmade park
After the railings and shrubberies
The birds the grass the trees the lake
And the wild boys innocent as strawberries
Had followed the hunchback
To his kennel in the dark.

In My Craft or Sullen Art

In my craft or sullen art
Exercised in the still night
When only the moon rages
And the lovers lie abed
With all their griefs in their arms,
I labour by singing light
Not for ambition or bread
Or the strut and trade of charms
On the ivory stages
But for the common wages
Of their most secret heart.

Not for the proud man apart
From the raging moon I write
On these spindrift pages
Nor for the towering dead
With their nightingales and psalms
But for the lovers, their arms
Round the griefs of the ages,
Who pay no praise or wages
Nor heed my craft or art.

Fern Hill

Now as I was young and easy under the apple boughs
About the lilting house and happy as the grass was green,
        The night above the dingle starry,
            Time let me hail and climb
        Golden in the heydays of his eyes,
And honoured among wagons I was prince of the apple towns
And once below a time I lordly had the trees and leaves
            Trail with daisies and barley
        Down the rivers of the windfall light.

And as I was green and carefree, famous among the barns
About the happy yard and singing as the farm was home,
        In the sun that is young once only,
            Time let me play and be
        Golden in the mercy of his means,
And green and golden I was huntsman and herdsman, the calves

Sang to my horn, the foxes on the hills barked clear and cold,
    And the sabbath rang slowly
      In the pebbles of the holy streams.

All the sun long it was running, it was lovely, the hay
Fields high as the house, the tunes from the chimneys, it was air
    And playing, lovely and watery
      And fire green as grass.
    And nightly under the simple stars
As I rode to sleep the owls were bearing the farm away,
All the moon long I heard, blessed among stables, the night-jars
    Flying with the ricks, and the horses
      Flashing into the dark.

And then to awake, and the farm, like a wanderer white
With the dew, come back, the cock on his shoulder: it was all
    Shining, it was Adam and maiden,
      The sky gathered again
    And the sun grew round that very day.
So it must have been after the birth of the simple light
In the first, spinning place, the spellbound horses walking warm
    Out of the whinnying green stable
      On to the fields of praise.

And honoured among foxes and pheasants by the gay house
Under the new made clouds and happy as the heart was long,
    In the sun born over and over,
      I ran my heedless ways,
    My wishes raced through the house high hay
And nothing I cared, at my sky blue trades, that time allows
In all his tuneful turning so few and such morning songs
    Before the children green and golden
      Follow him out of grace,

Nothing I cared, in the lamb white days, that time would take me
Up to the swallow thronged loft by the shadow of my hand,
    In the moon that is always rising,
      Nor that riding to sleep
    I should hear him fly with the high fields
And wake to the farm forever fled from the childless land.
Oh as I was young and easy in the mercy of his means,
      Time held me green and dying
    Though I sang in my chains like the sea.

Do Not Go Gentle Into That Good Night

Do not go gentle into that good night,
Old age should burn and rave at close of day;
Rage, rage against the dying of the light.

Though wise men at their end know dark is right,
Because their words had forked no lightning they
Do not go gentle into that good night.

Good men, the last wave by, crying how bright
Their frail deeds might have danced in a green bay,
Rage, rage against the dying of the light.

Wild men who caught and sang the sun in flight,
And learn, too late, they grieved it on its way,
Do not go gentle into that good night.

Grave men, near death, who see with blinding sight
Blind eyes could blaze like meteors and be gay,
Rage, rage against the dying of the light.

And you, my father, there on the sad height,
Curse, bless, me now with your fierce tears, I pray.
Do not go gentle into that good night.
Rage, rage against the dying of the light.

Over Sir John's Hill

Over Sir John's hill,
The hawk on fire hangs still;
In a hoisted cloud, at drop of dusk, he pulls to his claws
And gallows, up the rays of his eyes the small birds of the bay
And the shrill child's play
Wars
Of the sparrows and such who swansing, dusk, in wrangling
    hedges.
And blithely they squawk
To fiery tyburn over the wrestle of elms until
The flash the noosed hawk
Crashes, and slowly the fishing holy stalking heron
In the river Towy below bows his tilted headstone.

Flash, and the plumes crack,
And a black cap of jack-
Daws Sir John's just hill dons, and again the gulled birds hare
To the hawk on fire, the halter height, over Towy's fins,
In a whack of wind.
There
Where the elegiac fisherbird stabs and paddles
In the pebbly dab-filled
Shallow and sedge, and, 'dilly dilly,' calls the loft hawk,
'Come and be killed,'
I open the leaves of the water at a passage
Of psalms and shadows among the pincered sandcrabs prancing

And hear, in a shell,
Death clear as a buoy's bell:
All praise of the hawk on fire in hawk-eyed dusk be sung,
When his viperish fuse-hangs looped with flames under the
     brand
Wing, and blest shall
Young
Green chickens of the bay and bushes cluck, 'dilly dilly,
Come let us die.'
We grieve as the blithe birds, never again, leave shingle and elm,
The heron and I,
I young Aesop fabling to the near night by the dingle
Of eels, saint heron hymning in the distant

Crystal harbour vale
Where the sea cobbles sail,
And wharves of water where the walls dance and the white
     cranes stilt.
It is the heron and I, under judging Sir John's elmed
Hill, tell-tale the knelled
Guilt
Of the led-astray birds whom God, for their breast of whistles,
Have mercy on,
God in his whirlwind silence save, who marks the sparrows' hail,
For their souls' song.
Now the heron grieves in the weeded verge. Through windows
Of dusk and water I see the tilting whispering
Heron, mirrored, go,
As the snapt feathers snow,

Fishing in the tear of the Towy. Only a hoot owl
Hollows, a grassblade blown in cupped hands, in the looted elms
And no green cocks or hens
Shouts
Now on Sir John's hill. The heron, ankling the scaly
Lowlands of the waves,
Makes all the music; and I who hear the tune of the slow,
Wear-willow river, grave,
Before the lunge of the night, the notes on this time-shaken
Stone for the sake of the souls of the slain birds sailing.

ALUN LEWIS
All Day It Has Rained …

All day it has rained, and we on the edge of the moors
Have sprawled in our bell-tents, moody and dull as boors,
Groundsheets and blankets spread on the muddy ground
And from the first grey wakening we have found
No refuge from the skirmishing fine rain
And the wind that made the canvas heave and flap
And the taut wet guy-ropes ravel out and snap.
All day the rain has glided, wave and mist and dream,
Drenching the gorse and heather, a gossamer stream
Too light to stir the acorns that suddenly
Snatched from their cups by the wild south-westerly
Pattered against the tent and our upturned dreaming faces.
And we stretched out, unbuttoning our braces,
Smoking a Woodbine, darning dirty socks,
Reading the Sunday papers — I saw a fox
And mentioned it in the note I scribbled home; —
And we talked of girls, and dropping bombs on Rome,
And thought of the quiet dead and the loud celebrities
Exhorting us to slaughter, and the herded refugees;
— Yet thought softly, morosely of them, and as indifferently
As of ourselves or those whom we
For years have loved, and will again
To-morrow maybe love; but now it is the rain
Possesses us entirely, the twilight and the rain.

And I can remember nothing dearer or more to my heart
Than the children I watched in the woods on Saturday
Shaking down burning chestnuts for the schoolyard's merry play,
Or the shaggy patient dog who followed me
By Sheet and Steep and up the wooded scree
To the Shoulder o' Mutton where Edward Thomas brooded long
On death and beauty — till a bullet stopped his song.

The Mountain over Aberdare

From this high quarried ledge I see
The place for which the Quakers once
Collected clothes, my father's home,
Our stubborn bankrupt village sprawled
In jaded dusk beneath its nameless hills;
The drab streets strung across the cwm,
Derelict workings, tips of slag
The gospellers and gamblers use
And children scrutting for the coal
That winter dole cannot purvey;
Allotments where the collier digs
While engines hack the coal within his brain;
Grey Hebron in a rigid cramp,
White cheap-jack cinema, the church
Stretched like a sow beside the stream;
And mourners in their Sunday best
Holding a tiny funeral, singing hymns
That drift insidious as the rain
Which rises from the steaming fields
And swathes about the skyline crags
Till all the upland gorse is drenched
And all the creaking mountain gates
Drip brittle tears of crystal peace;
And in a curtained parlour women hug
Huge grief, and anger against God.

But now the dusk, more charitable than Quakers,
Veils the cracked cottages with drifting may
And rubs the hard day off the slate.
The colliers squatting on the ashtip
Listen to one who holds them still with tales,
While that white frock that floats down the dark alley

Looks just like Christ; and in the lane
The clink of coins among the gamblers
Suggests the thirty pieces of silver.

I watch the clouded years
Rune the rough foreheads of these moody hills,
This wet evening, in a lost age.

Goodbye

So we must say Goodbye, my darling,
And go, as lovers go, for ever;
Tonight remains, to pack and fix on labels
And make an end of lying down together.

I put a final shilling in the gas,
And watch you slip your dress below your knees
And lie so still I hear your rustling comb
Modulate the autumn in the trees.

And all the countless things I shall remember
Lay mummy-cloths of silence round my head;
I fill the carafe with a drink of water;
You say 'We paid a guinea for this bed,'

And then, 'We'll leave some gas, a little warmth
For the next resident, and these dry flowers,'
And turn your face away, afraid to speak
The big word, that Eternity is ours.

Your kisses close my eyes and yet you stare
As though God struck a child with nameless fears;
Perhaps the water glitters and discloses
Time's chalice and its limpid useless tears.

Everything we renounce except our selves;
Selfishness is the last of all to go;
Our sighs are exhalations of the earth,
Our footprints leave a track across the snow.

We made the universe to be our home,
Our nostrils took the wind to be our breath,

Our hearts are massive towers of delight,
We stride across the seven seas of death.

Yet when all's done you'll keep the emerald
I placed upon your finger in the street;
And I will keep the patches that you sewed
On my old battledress tonight, my sweet.

The Mahratta Ghats

The valleys crack and burn, the exhausted plains
Sink their black teeth into the horny veins
Straggling the hills' red thighs, the bleating goats —
— Dry bents and bitter thistles in their throats —
Thread the loose rocks by immemorial tracks.
Dark peasants drag the sun upon their backs.

High on the ghat the new turned soil is red,
The sun has ground it to the finest red,
It lies like gold within each horny hand.
Siva has spilt his seed upon this land.

Will she who burns and withers on the plain
Leave, ere too late, her scraggy herds of pain,
The cow-dung fire and the trembling beasts,
The little wicked gods, the grinning priests,
And climb, before a thousand years have fled,
High as the eagle to her mountain bed
Whose soil is fine as flour and blood-red?

But no! She cannot move. Each arid patch
Owns the lean folk who plough and scythe and thatch
Its grudging yield and scratch its stubborn stones.
The small gods suck the marrow from their bones.

Who is it climbs the summit of the road?
Only the beggar bumming his dark load.
Who was it cried to see the falling star?
Only the landless soldier lost in war.

And did a thousand years go by in vain?
And does another thousand start again?

Karanje Village

The sweeper said Karanje had a temple
A roof of gold in the gaon:
But I saw only the long-nosed swine and the vultures
Groping the refuse for carrion,
And the burial cairns on the hill with its spout of dust
Where the mules stamp and graze,
The naked children begging, the elders in poverty,
The sun's dry beat and glaze,

The crumbling hovels like a discredited fortress,
The old hags mumbling by the well,
The young girls in purple always avoiding us,
The monkeys loping obscenely round our smell —

— The trees were obscene with the monkeys' grey
   down-hanging
Their long slow leaping and stare,
The girl in a red sari despairingly swinging her rattle,
The sacred monkeys mocking all her care.

And alone by a heap of stones in the lonely salt plain
A little Vishnu of stone,
Silently and eternally simply Being,
Bidding me come alone,

And never entirely turning me away,
But warning me still of the flesh
That catches and limes the singing birds of the soul
And holds their wings in mesh.

But the people are hard and hungry and have no love
Diverse and alien, uncertain in their hate,
Hard stones flung out of Creation's silent matrix,
And the Gods must wait.
And Love must wait, as the unknown yellow poppy
Whose lovely fragile petals are unfurled
Among the lizards in this wasted land.

And when my sweetheart calls me shall I tell her
That I am seeking less and less of world?
And will she understand?

ALUN LEWIS

The Peasants

The dwarf barefooted, chanting
Behind the oxen by the lake,
Stepping lightly and lazily among the thorntrees
Dusky and dazed with sunlight, half awake;

The women breaking stones upon the highway,
Walking erect with burdens on their heads,
One body growing in another body,
Creation touching verminous straw beds.

Across scorched hills and trampled crops
The soldiers straggle by.
History staggers in their wake.
The peasants watch them die.

In Hospital: Poona (I)

Last night I did not fight for sleep
But lay awake from midnight while the world
Turned its slow features to the moving deep
Of darkness, till I knew that you were furled,

Beloved, in the same dark watch as I.
And sixty degrees of longitude beside
Vanished as though a swan in ecstasy
Had spanned the distance from your sleeping side.

And like to swan or moon the whole of Wales
Glided within the parish of my care:
I saw the green tide leap on Cardigan,
Your red yacht riding like a legend there,

And the great mountains, Dafydd and Llewelyn,
Plynlimmon, Cader Idris and Eryri
Threshing the darkness back from head and fin,
And also the small nameless mining valley

Whose slopes are scratched with streets and sprawling graves
Dark in the lap of firwoods and great boulders
Where you lay waiting, listening to the waves —
My hot hands touched your white despondent shoulders

— And then ten thousand miles of daylight grew
Between us, and I heard the wild daws crake
In India's starving throat; whereat I knew
That Time upon the heart can break
But love survives the venom of the snake.

The Sentry

I have begun to die.
For now at last I know
That there is no escape
From Night. Not any dream
Nor breathless images of sleep
Touch my bat's-eyes. I hang
Leathery-arid from the hidden roof
Of Night, and sleeplessly
I watch within Sleep's province.
I have left
The lovely bodies of the boy and girl
Deep in each other's placid arms;
And I have left
The beautiful lanes of sleep
That barefoot lovers follow to this last
Cold shore of thought I guard.
I have begun to die
And the guns' implacable silence
Is my black interim, my youth and age,
In the flower of fury, the folded poppy,
Night.

ROLAND MATHIAS
Porth Cwyfan

June, but the morning's cold, the wind
Bluffing occasional rain. I am clear
What brings me here across the stone
Spit to the island, but not what I shall find
When the dried fribbles of seaweed
Are passed, the black worked into the sandgrains
By the tide's mouthing. I can call nothing my own.

A closed-in, comfortless bay, the branchy
Shifts of voyage everywhere. On a slope
Of sand reaching up to the hidden
Field or stretch of marram a tipwhite, paunchy
Terrier sits pat on his marker, yapping me
Bodily out of range. What in God's name is he
Guarding that he thinks I want of a sudden?

To the left is the island, granite-hulled
Against froth, the chapel's roof acute
As Cwyfan put it when the finer
Passions ruled, convergent answers belled
Wetherlike towards God. Ahead is the cliff
Eaten by sand. On the quaking field beyond
Low huts, ordered and menacing. Porth China.

Once on the island those last shingle
Feet I came by seem in threat.
Can you, like Beuno, knit me back severed
Heads, Cwyfan, bond men to single
Living? Your nave has a few wild settles
And phantasmagoric dust. And Roger Parry,
Agent to Owen Bold, has a stone skew-whiff in the yard.

Doubling back again is a small
Inevitable tragedy, the umpteenth
In a sinuous month. Now I avoid
The violent pitch of the dog, with all
And nothing to guard, remark his croup,
The hysteric note in the bark. Two dunlin,
Huffing on long legs, pick in and out of the tide.

A man on the beach, a woman
And child with a red woollen cap,
Hummock and stop within earshot,
Eyeing my blundering walk. 'Can
We get to the island?', he asks, Lancashire
Accent humble, dark curls broad. And I
Am suddenly angry. But how is my tripright sounder,
Save that I know Roger Parry and he does not?

Sanderlings

That plump little chorus
Tripping balletically,
Leaning delicately into the gale
With the daft precision
Of a collective toy,
Was wound up with a skein
From the ice-cap. This
Is the rude Ardudwy
Station: some skill in
Diplomacy compels
These spasms of wittering,
The tiny side-stepping
Runs that carry the watcher
From foam to deliquescent
Foam and no further, since
The wind postpones take-off
And the chorus ticked in
At Murmansk must whir
Till the Orange River
Groans like a lighthouse
In the craw of survivors.
Naïve of us, then, to cry
Strangers: for a storm in Wales
Trims their flight, not
Their purposes, and wise
We should know whose birds
By right sing here
Before clapping these travellers
Welcome.

Cae Iago: May Day

Among these arthritic contours,
Little atlas and himalaya
Dip down to cwms of glaciered pasture
And stiffen, back to the bluff
Of a new rigidity. Most of the old
Walls have fallen, the blackthorn
Splushes have grown out, and each
Of the half enclosures has its
Happy trackway up or on behind

That outburst of rock, beyond
This bracken hill. Cock
Pheasants walk these broken
Enclosures, their picking step
Unharassed. The sheep have their
Winter coats round their ears
And the lambs making play by
Tree roots limber and jump
On each other in the brief
Seconds that sun has
To manoeuvre the clouds away.

It is all new! It is not just
Spring hiding behind the snow showers
Or the damson budding again
From its fungused bark. Over
The vanquished summits Ieuan
Appears, his big-wheeled Honda
Trike pursued by sheep, or at
Feeding time rattles a tractor
Down improbable slopes, unbagging
Beet-pulp nuts in trail along
Some shelf of grass, keeping
The hollow bricks of ochred
Minerals topped up. The old
Nomad was right. What has the air
Of cities but obstruction and
The hospital breath of in-fighting?
Up here the men are dead
Who might have argued and the world
Goes on. Snow slants between
This window and Hafotty Ganol's
Ruin across the cwm: the pheasant
Makes his parade: surviving man
Roars up the bounds of his latest kingdom.

Grasshoppers

What is it to grasp,
From this moment, this hasty
Bolt of food on the Rhinerhorn
Where the wimberries thin out

And the few stunts of spruce have
Already reckoned with winter? Patently
It is the grasshoppers I
Must listen to, as they intersperse
A hard leg-music with mad
Travels from tussock to bleaker
Tuft, to broken stick or random
Protuberant stone. Some of these
Rakish frames hark back lime-
Green in talk, some converse
In brown or blue. But every one
Presently makes hard music in
A stop in this Indian summer of his,
Knowing there's no survival
Except in the eggs that instinct
Buried in the entablature at the
Inevitable season. Rightness
Is not in question. It is plainly
Right, here where the trees
On the contour are ellipses, faint
And separate in the transverse sun
Stretching to the strict blue ridge
They will never attain, it is right
To climb as we can, to the limit
Of will. To do less
Is unworthy of such sun, such far
Blue purpose as the distance is,
Folded back and back, fainter
And fainter always, surpassing
Peak with peak, till the day
Is what we can never be and scarcely comprehend.

EMYR HUMPHREYS
From Father to Son

There is no limit to the number of times
Your father can come to life, and he is as tender as ever he was
And as poor, his overcoat buttoned to the throat,
His face blue from the wind that always blows in the outer
  darkness

He comes towards you, hesitant,
Unwilling to intrude and yet driven at the point of love
To this encounter.

You may think
That love is all that is left of him, but when he comes
He comes with all his winters and all his wounds.
He stands shivering in the empty street,
Cold and worn like a tramp at the end of a journey
And yet a shape of unquestioning love that you
Uneasy and hesitant of the cold touch of death
Must embrace.

Then, before you can touch him
He is gone, leaving on your fingers
A little more of his weariness
A little more of his love.

JOHN STUART WILLIAMS
Early Days

One evening, when gorse was burning
on back-drop hills and the low sun
set slate and stone on fire,
I sat at my high window watching
the long lane up from town
lacing the terraced houses to the pit.
At its far end a loyal servant,
no honest man, turned into its shortcut
mouth. He hesitated, seemed alone
and frightened, the path narrowing before him,
then, with a glance behind, pressed
on. At each yard's end
shadows became waiting men.
Some puffed coltsfoot as they watched,
others dragged on cigarettes. One,
I remember, held in his hands a sprig
of elder-flower. So many eyes,
yet his saw only the stubbing stones.
Nothing was said. Only the gulls

and the blackleg shunters in the yard below
pushed out of silence. Half way,
pitboots slipping on the heavy shale,
he managed not to run as the narrow
lane became one of the lost places
of the world and day stopped its breath.
At last, just before the anxious
sergeant showed his blue serge
round the far corner, he made it.
Grandfather took his pipe from his mouth,
looked at it and spat carefully between
his feet and the watching men became
again the easy friends and butties
we all knew. Gently casual
words let in ordinary
day. One wag said,
'Broke his bloody record today!
Think he'll make the Powderhall?'
No one answered. Each man
knows his own longest journey.

Rhyfel y Sais Bach

As a result of enclosures of common land in Cardiganshire, one Augustus
Brackenbury, 'the little Englishman', purchased some 850 acres or so
towards the end of 1819 and, the following year, proceeded to build a
house. There was much local resentment, perhaps because the ground
enclosed was where the local people had been accustomed to cut peat.

The Complaint of Augustus Brackenbury

My Lord, I take the liberty of submitting a case
peculiar in hardship, not from single malice
but from the Disposition of the body of People
from which, it seems, there cannot be redress.

Some time since, you ordered troops
against the Peasantry resisting rightful enclosure
of lands lying waste in the Lordship of Mevenidd
in Cardigan County. Yet now, after a lapse

of three years only, I am subject to the same
violence rendered more daring by impunity

and more malignant through being directed against
a man they call a stranger, English tho' I am.

I have done my duty, properly sought to improve
my Property by fencing, cultivation and building,
intending nothing but the betterment of all;
but in little more than a year, five

times have buildings been destroyed, in spite
of all precaution, by Mobs, disguised and armed —
stones have been thrown, shots fired, and
I regret to say, my life placed under threat.

Information on Oath has been countered by the most
unblushing perjury supported in their fixity of purpose
by an Opinion that the Magistrates of the Country
appear not cordial in their desire to do what's best

to bring the Offenders to Justice. This cause
renders useless all attempts at redress;
and unless your Lordships listen to my plea I shall
be deprived of a valuable Property by lawless force.

I subjoin an Appendix in which I name names
and recount circumstance, and a shameful letter
threatening me and my 'Sentry Boys' further
visitation. We are not safe in our homes,

this letter signed 'Paddies' but writ
in the hand of one James Morris, formerly
a Clergyman of the Established Church but unfrocked
thro' ill conduct; he is at liberty yet.

That the land is colonised by Strangers is true;
and they appear unused to the law of trespass:
there is also some talk of ancient rights
of turbary: but these things said, I know

Your Lordships will see it plain: an Englishman alone,
conspired against, lacking the Law's support
amongst false swearers and mean conspirators.
Send back the soldiers and have done.

What wrong have I, that these I only
wished to help have treated me so? I humbly
beseech your earnest consideration. Yours
in supplication, Augustus Brackenbury.

HARRI WEBB
Pastoral

You see that forest on the height?
They say it hides a town
Where flaring forges banished night.
Do they? Let's sit down.

You see that valley at our feet
So green and wild to see?
They say it once was one long street.
What's that to you and me?

And where your father's sheep now graze
And where I drive the plough
Tall chimneys rose in olden days.
Let's sit closer now.

And in that town the people all
Esteemed themselves so wise
They thought their place would never fall.
Haven't you got nice eyes.

And all those people of our race
Gone now beneath our farms,
Such silence in the busy place.
Hold me in your arms.

Epil y Filiast

Already something of a stranger now
A spry old man is walking his milgi out
Of a Sunday morning when the nineteenth century
Is in chapel and the twentieth in bed.

But his morning is centuries younger than these
As he steps it out and the lean dog lopes beside him
To fields where it will flash and pounce and double
As once in Glyn Cuch Woods.
And the old man stands in his grubby mackintosh
With a jaunty set to his shoulders,
A clean white scarf around his withered throat
And his cap on one side — *ticyn slic*.
His whistle carries further than the rotting pitheads,
The grass-grown tips, the flashy, flimsy estates.
He is a gambler, a drinker, a doggy-boy,
Better at drawing the dole than earning a wage.
The supermarket rises where Calfaria stood,
To him it is all one, he is older than any of it.
Mark him well, he is the last of his kind,
The last heir of Cadwaladr, Caswallon
And all our dead princes.

The Nightingales

Once there were none and the dark air was dumb
Over the tree-stumps, the bare deforested hills.
They were a legend that the old bards had sung,
Gone now, like so much, so much.
But once I heard them drilling away the dark,
Llandâf was loud with them all of a summer's night
And the great Garth rose like a rock from their storm.
This most of all I desire: to hear the nightingales
Not by Taff only but by all our streams,
Black Rhymni, sullen Ogwr, dirty Ebbw
Dishonoured Tawe and all our sewered drabs.
And others whose names are an unvisited music
(Wales, Wales, who can know all your rivers?)
The nightingales singing beyond the Teifi,
By Aeron, Ystwyth, Rheidol, and those secret waters
The Beacons hold: Rhiangoll, Tarrell, Crawnon,
By Hepste and Mellte outstanding Scwd Einion Gam
(But let them not sing by Elan, Claerwen, Fyrnwy
Or Tryweryn of the Shame.)
You who have outsung all our dead poets,
Sing for them again in Cwm Prysor and Dyffryn Ceiriog,

And humble Gwydderig and Creidiol, do not forget them.
And that good man, no poet, who gave us a song
Even sweeter than yours, sing for him at Llanrhaeadr,
And in Glyndyfrdwy, what need to tell you to sing?
Sing in the faded lands, Maelienydd and Elfael,
And in the plundered cantrefs that have no name.
Come back and sing to us, we have waited too long,
For too long have not been worth singing for.
The magic birds that sang for heroes in Harlech
And hushed to wonder the wild Ardudwy sea
And they of Safaddan that sing only for princes,
We cannot call them again, but come you
And fill our hearts like the hearts of other men.
Shall we hear you again soon, soon?

Synopsis of the Great Welsh Novel

Dai K lives at the end of a valley. One is not quite sure
Whether it has been drowned or not. His Mam
Loves him too much and his Dada drinks.
As for his girlfriend Blodwen, she's pregnant. So
Are all the other girls in the village — there's been a Revival.
After a performance of Elijah, the mad preacher
Davies the Doom has burnt the chapel down.
One Saturday night after the dance at the Con Club,
With the Free Wales Army up to no good in the back-lanes,
A stranger comes to the village; he is, of course,
God, the well known television personality. He succeeds
In confusing the issue, whatever it is, and departs
On the last train before the line is closed.
The colliery blows up, there is a financial scandal
Involving all the most respected citizens; the Choir
Wins at the National. It is all seen, naturally,
Through the eyes of a sensitive boy who never grows up.
The men emigrate to America, Cardiff and the moon. The girls
Find rich and foolish English husbands. Only daft Ianto
Is left to recite the Complete Works of Sir Lewis Morris
To puzzled sheep, before throwing himself over
The edge of the abandoned quarry. One is not quite sure
Whether it is fiction or not.

Ode to the Severn Bridge

Two lands at last connected
Across the waters wide
And all the tolls collected
On the English side.

Vive Le Sport

Sing a song of rugby,
Buttocks, booze and blood,
Thirty dirty ruffians
Brawling in the mud.

When the match is over,
They're at the bar in throngs,
If you think the game is filthy,
Then you should hear the songs.

Cywydd o Fawl
(yn null y gogogynfeirdd à gogo)

Flap we our lips, praise Big Man,
Bards religious shire Cardigan.
Not frogs croaking are we
Nor vain crows but bards tidy.
Wise is our speak, like Shadrach,
Hearken you now, people bach.
Mouth some, Cardiff ach y fi,
Not holy like Aberteifi.
Twp it is to speech so,
In Cardiff is gold yellow,
Truth it is and no fable,
All for bards respectable.
White Jesus bach, let no ill
Befall Big Heads Arts Council.
Pounds they have, many thousand,
Like full till shop draper grand.
Good is the work they are at,
Soaped they shall be in Seiat,

Reserved shall be for them
A place in Big Seat Salem.
Praised let them be for this thing,
Money they are distributing
Like Beibl Moses his manna.
Tongue we all, bards Welsh, Ta!

ROBERT MORGAN
Blood Donor

The searching was easy and memory ripens
On the grey earth picture of Rees
In his grimy vest soaked in blood.
Forty-eight years under tense rock
Had stripped him like a naked tree with roots
In slag and marked him with texture of strain
And accident. But it was slow legs
And dust-worn eyes that were to blame.

The iron rock-bar was still in his hands
Held like a spear of a fallen warrior.
The rocks had dyed his silver hair red
And the heavy bar was warm and worn.
Blind flies swarmed in the blood-sweat
Air and the tough men with bruised
Senses were gentle, using distorted
Hands like women arranging flowers.

On the way out, through twisting roads of rocky
Silence, you could sense images of confusion
In the slack chain of shadows; muscles
Were nerve-tight and thoughts infested
With wrath and sharp edges of fear.
Towards the sun's lamp we moved, taking
Home the dark prisoner in his shroud of coats.

T.H. JONES

My Grandmother Died in the Early Hours of the Morning

It was cold in that room, after the cold hours
Of keeping company with the big, shrunk man
Who had been her husband, my father's father.
Her sallow face seemed peaceful as ever,
Her straggle of hair blanched into the pillow
— You would not have guessed at a body under the bedclothes.
Past tiredness, I was a boy, incurious.
A little woman was dead, a little old woman
Who had long confused me with her youngest son.
I did not even think, How small she looks.
And certainly had no thoughts for her life of labour,
Nor wondered how she who had always been old to me
Had once been whatever beauty the world has
To the old man I now led out of the room,
Out of the house, up the narrow road,
In the dawn he could not see for tears, taking
My hand in his as he'd done when I was small,
Both of us wordless against the dawn and death.

A Storm in Childhood

We had taken the long way home, a mile
Or two further than any of us had to walk,
But it meant being together longer, and home later.

The storm broke on us — broke is a cliché,
But us isn't — that storm was loosed for us, on us.
My cousin Blodwen, oldest and wisest of us,
Said in a voice we'd never heard her use before:
'The lightning kills you when it strikes the trees.'
If we were in anything besides a storm, it was trees.
On our left, the valley bottom was nothing but trees,
And on our right the trees went halfway up
The hill. We ran, between the trees and the trees,
Five children hand-in-hand, afraid of God,
Afraid of being among the lightning-fetching
Trees, soaked, soaked with rain, with sweat, with tears,
Frightened, if that's the adequate word, frightened
By the loud voice and the lambent threat,

Frightened certainly of whippings for being late,
Five children, ages six to eleven, stumbling
After a bit of running through trees from God.
Even my cousin who was eleven — I can't remember
If she was crying, too — I suppose I hope so.
But I do remember the younger ones when the stumbling
Got worse as the older terror of trees got worse
Adding their tears' irritation to the loud world of wet
And tall trees waiting to be struck by the flash, and us
With them — that running stumble, hand-in-hand — five
Children aware of our sins as we ran stumblingly:
Our sins which seemed such pointless things to talk
About to mild Miss Davies on the hard Sunday benches.
The lightning struck no trees, nor any of us.
I think we all got beaten; some of us got colds.

It was the longest race I ever ran,
A race against God's voice sounding from the hills
And his blaze aimed at the trees and at us,
A race in the unfriendly rain, with only the other
Children, hand-in-hand, to comfort me to know
They too were frightened, all of us miserable sinners.

Back?
(to R.S. Thomas)

Back is the question
Carried to me on the curlew's wing,
And the strong sides of the salmon.

Should I go back then
To the narrow path, the sheep turds,
And the birded language?

Back to an old, thin bitch
Fawning on my spit, writhing
Her lank belly with memories:

Back to the chapel, and a charade
Of the word of God made by a preacher
Without a tongue:

Back to the ingrowing quarrels,
The family where you have to remember
Who is not speaking to whom:

Back to the shamed memories of Glyndŵr
And Saunders Lewis's aerodrome
And a match at Swansea?

Of course I'd go back if somebody'd pay me
To live in my own country
Like a bloody Englishman.

But for now, lacking the money,
I must be content with the curlew's cry
And the salmon's taut belly

And the waves, of water and of fern
And words, that beat unendingly
On the rocks of my mind's country.

Mr Jones as the Transported Poet
(for Gwen)

'And how do you react to exile?' Politely
They ask; and remnants of my country courtesy
Make me answer politely, meaninglessly.

I say, 'Of course, a poet is in exile
Anywhere, always.' And that 'of course' disarms,
Undoes them. They are politely satisfied.
There was something they always knew about poets.

Or I say, putting on a bit more accent,
And of course prefacing what I have to say
With that disarming and dishonest 'of course'.
I say, 'Of course, we Welshmen are exiles
Just as much in England as Australia.'
And they nod understandingly and smile politely,
And think I didn't really understand the question.

How could I tell them, politely or impolitely,
That the only exile is from her bed,

From that visionary and impossible moment
When our customary involvement made
A sudden meaning we had not known before?

Exile, like love, is a word not to be lightly said.

Bird on a Jaunt

Hours ago he woke up the sky,
Has eaten well, now walks about
The kingdom of his confidence,
Feels good, his strong legs
Spur the ground, his neck
Tenses, and he crows again,
A cheer, a challenge,
Just for the hell of it, the gold
Cry vibrant to the horizon,
To the top of the sky, is conscious
Of the sheen of his wings, feels good
This blue morning he has called
Into being, now blesses,
And suddenly purposeful
Strides, pounces, jerks
His mien and mastery
Into the nearest compliant,
Inoffensive brown novice
Of his service, dismounts,
And walks away in the disdain
Of feeling really good this morning.

LESLIE NORRIS
Elegy for Lyn James

I saw your manager fight. He was
Useful, but his brother had the class.
In shabby halls in Wales, or in tents
On slum ground, I saw your like
Go cuffed and bleeding from a few
Crude rounds to set the mob aloud
Before the big men came, who had the class.

Even they did not all escape. Tim
Sheehan, whose young heart burst
In a dirty room above a fish shop;
Jerry O'Neill bobbing his old age
Through a confusion of scattered
Fists all down the High Street; brisk
Billy Rose, blind; all these I knew.

And Jock McAvoy, swinging his right
From a wheel-chair. Your murderers hide
Fatly behind the black lines of the
Regulations, your futile hands are closed
In a gloveless death. In rotting lanes
Behind silent billiard halls, I hear
Your shuffling ghost, who never had the class.

Hyperion

was hardly a Titan. He stood
a brief inch over six feet, was
sweetly made. Not for his size
am I sent in his just praise
along the measured tracks

of his achievement. Dropped
on the printed turf by Selene,
daughter of Serenissima, he moved
even in his first uncertainty
like one waited for. His birth

was in green April, and he grew
in light, on the fat meadows.
Gently schooled, he delighted
his mentors with his perfect ardour,
honesty, the speed of his response.

Though small, he was quite beautiful,
his chestnut mane burning, his step
luminous. Some doubted his courage,
looking askance at the delicacy
of his white feet, ignoring the star

already brilliant in his forehead.
His heart was a vivid instrument
drumming for victory, loin and muscle
could stretch and flex in eating
leaps. When he ran, when he ran

the rings of his nostrils were scarlet,
the white foam spun away from his lips.
For his was the old, true blood,
untainted in his veins' walls:
two lines to St Simon, two lines

to Bend Or: The Flying Dutchman,
Bayardo, Galopin, all the great ones
back in his pedigree met in him.
He could not fail to honour
his fathers in the proud flood

of his winning. Nine times he left
his crescent grooves in the cheering
grass before the commoners gasped
after him. At Epsom, racing as if
alone on the classic track, he won

a record Derby, at Doncaster the Leger.
He won the Chester Vase, the Prince
of Wales's Stakes. Nor in his fullness,
drowsing in quiet fields in quiet company,
was he forgotten. His children,

sons and daughters of the Sun,
did not allow this. Hypericum,
Sun Chariot, Rising Light, all
were his. And Sun Stream, Midas,
Owen Tudor, Suncastle, many others.

The swift Godiva was his, and in
his image famous Citation, who ran
away with all America. Sportsmen,
all who go to the races, who marvel
at the flying hooves, remember Hyperion.

His Father, Singing

My father sang for himself,
out of sadness and poverty;
perhaps from happiness,
but I'm not sure of that.

He sang in the garden,
quietly, a quiet voice
near his wallflowers
which of all plants

he loved most, calling them
gillyflowers, a name
learned from his mother.
His songs came from a time

before my time, his boy's
life among musical brothers,
keeping pigeons, red and blue
checkers, had a racing cycle

with bamboo wheels. More often
he sang the songs he'd learned,
still a boy, up to his knees
in French mud, those dying songs.

He sang for us once only,
our mother away from the house,
the lamp lit, and I reading,
seven years old, already bookish,

at the scrubbed table.
My brother cried from his crib
in the small bedroom, teething,
a peremptory squall, then a long

wail. My father lifted from
the sheets his peevish child,
red-faced, feverish, carried
him down in a wool shawl

and in the kitchen, holding
the child close, began to sing.

Quietly, of course, and swaying
rhythmically from foot to foot,

he rocked the sobbing boy.
I saw my brother's head,
his puckered face, fall
on my father's chest. His crying

died away, and I
read on. It was my father's
singing brought my head up.
His little wordless lullabies

had gone, and what he sang
above his baby's sleep
was never meant
for any infant's comfort.

He stood in the bleak kitchen,
the stern, young man, my father.
For the first time raised
his voice, in pain and anger

sang. I did not know his song
nor why he sang it. But stood
in fright, knowing it important,
and someone should be listening.

A Glass Window, in Memory of Edward Thomas, at Eastbury Church

The road lay in moistening valleys, lanes
Awash with evening, expensive racehorses
Put to bed in pastures under the elms.
I was disappointed. Something in me turns

Urchin at so much formality, such pastoral
Harmony. I grumble for rock outcrops,
In filed, rasping country. The church drips
Gently, in perfect English, and we all

Troop in, see the lit window, smile, and look
Again; shake out wet coats. Under your name
The images of village, hill and home,
And crystal England stands against the dark.

The path cut in the pane most worries me,
Coming from nowhere, moving into nowhere.
Is it the road to the land no traveller
Tells of? I turn away, knowing it is, for me,

That sullen lane leading you out of sight,
In darkening France, the road taken.
Suddenly I feel the known world shaken
By gunfire, by glass breaking. In comes the night.

Bridges

Imagine the bridge launched, its one foot
Clamped hard on bedrock, and such grace
In its growth it resembles flying, is flight
Almost. It is not chance when they speak
Of throwing a bridge; it leaves behind a track
Of its parallel rise and fall, solid
In quarried stone, in timber, in milled
Alloy under stress. A bridge is

The path of flight. A friend, a soldier,
Built a laughable wartime bridge over
Some unknown river. In featureless night
He threw from each slid bank the images
Of his crossing, working in whispers, under
Failing lamps. As they built, braced spars,
Bolted taut the great steel plugs, he hoped
His bridge would stand in brawny daylight, complete,

The two halves miraculously knit. But
It didn't. Airily they floated above
Midstream, going nowhere, separate
Beginnings of different bridges, offering
The policies of inaction, neither coming
Nor going. His rough men cursed, sloped off,
Forded quite easily a mile lower.
It was shallow enough for his Land Rover.

I have a bridge over a stream. Four
Wooden sleepers, simple, direct. After rain,
Very slippery. I rarely cross right over,
Preferring to stand, watching the grain
On running water. I like such bridges best,
River bridges on which men always stand,
In quiet places. Unless I could have that other,
A bridge launched, hovering, wondering where to land.

Belonging

He came after the reading, when all
Had left, the students, the kind
Congratulating friends, and I was tired.

What it was gave me more than a
Public courtesy for this old man,
Small, neat in his blue suit, someone's

Grandfather, I can't say. He held
A paper faded as his eyes; his family
Tree. Anxious, erect, expecting my

Approval, he stood in the hot room.
'I'm Welsh,' he said. I read his
Pedigree. Bentley, Lawrence, Faulkner,

Graydon, no Welsh names. I nodded,
Gave back his folded pride, shook
My head in serious admiration. Belonging,

After all, is mostly a matter of belief.
'I should have known you anywhere,' I said,
'For a Welshman.' He put away his chart,

Shook hands, walked into the foreign light.
I watched him go. Outside, the sprinklers,
Waving their spraying rainbows, kept America green.

Hudson's Geese

'... I have, from time to time, related some incident of my
boyhood and these are contained in various chapters in *The
Naturalist in La Plata, Birds and Man, Adventures among
Birds...*'

W.H. Hudson, in *Far Away and Long Ago*.

Hudson tells us of them,
the two migrating geese,
she hurt in the wing
indomitably walking
the length of a continent,
and he wheeling above,
calling his distress.
They could not have lived.
Already I see her wing
scraped past the bone
as she drags it through rubble.
A fox, maybe, took her
in his snap jaws. And what
would he do, the point
of his circling gone?
The wilderness of his cry
falling through an air
turned instantly to winter
would warn the guns of him.
If a fowler dropped him,
let it have been quick,
pellets hitting brain
and heart so his weight
came down senseless,
and nothing but his body
to enter the dog's mouth.

Elegy for David Beynon

David, we must have looked comic, sitting
there at next desks; your legs stretched
half-way down the classroom, while
my feet hung a free inch above

the floor. I remember, too, down
at The Gwynne's Field, at the side
of the little Taff, dancing with
laughing fury as you caught

effortlessly at the line-out, sliding
the ball over my head direct to
the outside-half. That was Cyril
Theophilus, who died in his quiet

so long ago that only I, perhaps,
remember he'd hold the ball one-handed
on his thin stomach as he turned
to run. Even there you were careful

to miss us with your scattering
knees as you bumped through
for yet another try. Buffeted
we were, but cheered too by our

unhurt presumption in believing
we could ever have pulled you down.
I think those children, those who died
under your arms in the crushed school,

would understand that I make this
your elegy. I know the face you had,
have walked with you enough mornings
under the fallen leaves. Theirs is

the great anonymous tragedy one word
will summarise. Aberfan, I write it
for them here, knowing we've paid to it
our shabby pence, and now it can be stored

with whatever names there are where
children end their briefest pilgrimage.
I cannot find the words for you, David. These
are too long, too many; and not enough.

RUTH BIDGOOD
Little of Distinction

Little of distinction, guide-books had said —
a marshy common and a windy hill:
a renovated church, a few old graves
with curly stones and cherubs with blind eyes:
yews with split trunks straining at rusty bands:
and past the church, a house or two, a farm,
not picturesque, not even very old.
And yet, the day I went there, life that breaks
so many promises gave me a present
it had not promised — I found this place
had beauty after all. How could I have seen
how a verandah's fantastic curlicues
would throw a patterned shadow on the grass?
or thought how delicate ash-leaves would stir
against a sky of that young blue? or known
trees and grey walls would have such truthful beauty,
like an exact statement? And least of all
could I have foreseen the miles on hazy miles
of Radnorshire and Breconshire below,
uncertain in the heat — the mystery
that complements precision. So much sweeter
was this day than the expectation of it.

Old Pump-house, Llanwrtyd Wells

The door is open. I shall not be intruding,
going in to sit on the bench by the wall,
to breathe the stuffy dankness streaked with sulphur,
and stare through broken panes over the shaggy grounds.
This sociable place has died through lack of visiting.
A pungent drip, still slowly forced from the spring's heart,
has grown a fungus-garden in the great mirrored basin.
Some chairs lie on the sheep-fouled floor,
some lurch, still conversationally grouped,
against the counter over which was handed
health by the tumberful when crowds came here,
laughing and garrulous, to take the waters;
pulling faces over the taste of their cure,
and bragging of the glasses they had drunk

like boys about their beer. They came streaming
six times a day from the bursting village
to jostle and gossip round the sulphur-bar.
Sheep-farmers, knitting wives, holiday miners
from the black valleys, jam-packed the houses,
ate meals in shifts, and sat outside singing hymns
on the suddenly hushed street of evening;
or went back in warm dusk to the well-house
to hear the Builth harper play under summer trees
and watch the youngsters dance.
The plucked notes, never wholly gay, and laughing voices
spiralled up through the trees, up the long valley;
and lost themselves among the hills
over the sealed frontier of the past.

Safaddan

(Many stories are told of Llyn Safaddan — Llangorse Lake
— in Breconshire. The River Llynfi, which flows through
it, is said never to mingle its waters with those of the lake.
There are tales of a city buried under the lake. The birds
of Safaddan sing only for the rightful heir to the throne of
Wales. Giraldus says that three knights once put this
tradition to the test. The two Anglo-Normans got no re-
sponse to their commands, but for Gruffydd ap Rhys ap
Tewdwr every bird cried aloud and beat its wings.)

Through bruised reeds my boat thrusts
into open water. First light broke thin mist
and was broken in a scatter of brightness
on the grey lake. In the depths
Llynfi coursed, eternally separate,
spurning the lake-waters beyond
intangible banks of its own force.
Silent lay the drowned city of legend
with its aqueous colonnades.

I had never seen the lake so thronged with birds
or known them so quiet. Hundreds there were,
out on the water, on the island,
and secret among the reeds.
On the further shore, three horsemen

rode to the lake's edge. Two dismounted,
each in turn shouting over the water —
I could not hear the words. From all
that intricate pattern of stilled wings
and watchful eyes, not one bird startled up.
The shouting sank dully into the lake.

Now the third rider, tall on a tall white horse,
slowly paced down to the hushing waters,
dismounted, knelt in prayer. I shipped my oars
and was quiet as the birds. When he stood
in the growing sunlight, knowledge came to me.
I knelt in the boat. He called.

All round me, suddenly were wings
beating the water, rustling the reeds,
and a thousand songs of homage rose.
My boat rocked in the joyful surge
of Llynfi's invisible stream, my ears
were dazed with triumphant proclamations
of sunken bells, and louder and louder
the All Hails of Safaddan's birds.
Lake and kingly rider and host of birds,
and I with them, were caught up into the sun.

Fragmented sun on sliding water:
reed-beds thick at the lake's verge:
the island low astern. Three distant riders
dwindling on a path away from the shore.
Tired, I reached for the oars.
I had never seen so many birds
on the lake. They were lifting, one by one
or dense in wedge-shaped flights.
It was quiet. There was only
my oars' creak-and-plash
and the soft rush of departing wings.

Hawthorn at Digiff

When I was a child, hawthorn
was never brought into our house.
It was godless to throw a pinch

of spilled salt, or dodge ladders,
yet no-one ever carried in
the doomy sweetness of red may or white.

Down there by the river,
shivering with heat, is Digiff,
a house full of hawthorn. The tree
grows in the midst of it, glowing
with pale pink blossom, thrusting
through gaps that were windows,
reaching up where no roof
intervenes between hearth and sky.

On the hill, sun has hardened
old soggy fields below the bluebell woods.
Rusty wire sags from rotten posts.
Outcrops, couchant dinosaurs, share
rough comfort with a few unshorn sheep.
Below, gardens have left their mark.

I bring a thought into this day's light
of Esther and Gwen, paupers:
Rhys and Thomas, shepherds: John Jones,
miner of copper and lead:
who lived here and are not remembered,
whose valley is re-translated
by holiday bathers across the river,
lying sun-punched: by me:
by men who keep a scatter of sheep
on the old by-takes.

At Digiff is hawthorn on hearth and bed-place.
Seen close, the tree is flushed
with decay. Sick lichened branches
put out in desperate profusion
blossom that hardly knows
an hour of whiteness before slow dying
darkens it. This is that glowing tree
of doom and celebration,
whose cankered flowers I touch
gently, and go down to the ford.

Banquet

(At the time of the 19th-century religious revivals it was
said of two old North Breconshire women, 'The Revival
was a banquet for them.')

Their youth was poor and barren as the land.
The mould that should have formed them women
held some flaw, broke early
spilling them out to harden into things
men's eyes would never rest on
except with scorn.
                                    They were strong, though.
Fighting their stony patch
on its shelf of rock, they won.
The mound-encircled garden was rough, plain,
growing food, not flowers; yet as they touched
the juicy crispness of new sap-filled leaves
they learned a kind of tenderness.

By rushlight at the dark of the year,
when knitting-pins made winter music,
they could remember those great skies
spread lordly-wise above them when they wandered
hill-pastures, scratting grey tough wool
from fence and thorn.
                                    Year after year
came back thaw, singing, airy softness,
pulsing of the blood, to tease and mock,
then gale and fall of leaf and snow
to tell them what they knew too well.

Then, when they were almost old, he came.
He preached in the river-meadow
to crowds who wept and begged and leapt,
cried 'Glory, glory!', fell
foaming on the rough tussocks of grass.

He seemed to speak softly, yet from the hill
they heard, and from their hut came
fearfully, like unhandled ponies.
He looked up, smiled. They were unused to love.
This thing seemed other than the rut and musk

most knew (not they). Stumbling,
each clutching the other on the sliding stones,
they took the short cut down.

That was the start of it — their banqueting-time,
wine of God, and gold, and bath
of sweetest milk, damask tent
and bed of silk, lemon-grove,
low-hung moon, summer, subtle song,
their rest, their dawn, their piercing love.

The dark time came again. They rattled logs
into flame, and shadows walked the wall.
They grew old, hunched over the hearth.
One muttered words he taught,
the other joined her in prayer,
catching at the rags of a memory. Snow
sifted under the door. Each stretched her hands
to the fire, like a beggar,
and waited for the placing in her palm
of a small dole of love.

JOHN ORMOND
My Dusty Kinsfolk

My dusty kinsfolk in the hill
Screwed up in elm, when you were dead
We tucked you though your hands were still
In the best blanket from your bed
As though you dozed and might in stirring
Push off some light shroud you were wearing.

We did it against double cold,
Cold of your deaths and our own.
We placed you where a vein of coal
Can still be seen when graves are open.
The Dunvant seam spreads fingers in
The churchyard under Penybryn.

And so you lie, my fellow villagers,
In ones and twos and families
Dead behind Ebenezer. Jamjars
Carry flowers for you, but the trees
Put down their roots to you as surely as
You breath was not, and was, and was.

Early and lately dead, each one
Of you haunts me. Continue
To tenant the air where I walk in the sun
Beyond the shadow of yew.
I speak these words to you, my kin
And friends, in requiem and celebration.

My Grandfather and His Apple Tree

Life sometimes held such sweetness for him
As to engender guilt. From the night vein he'd come,
From working in water wrestling the coal,
Up the pit slant. Every morning hit him
Like a journey of trams between the eyes;
A wild and drinking farmboy sobered by love
Of a miller's daughter and a whitewashed cottage
Suddenly to pay rent for. So he'd left the farm
For dark under the fields six days a week
With mandrel and shovel and different stalls.
All light was beckoning. Soon his hands
Untangled a brown garden into neat greens.

There was an apple tree he limed, made sturdy;
The fruit was sweet and crisp upon the tongue
Until it budded temptation in his mouth.
Now he had given up whistling on Sundays,
Attended prayer-meetings, added a concordance
To his wedding Bible and ten children
To the village population. He nudged the line,
Clean-pinafored and collared, glazed with soap,
Every seventh day of rest in Ebenezer;
Shaved on a Saturday night to escape the devil.

The sweetness of the apples worried him.
He took a branch of cooker from a neighbour

When he became a deacon, wanting
The best of both his worlds. Clay from the colliery
He thumbed about the bole one afternoon
Grafting the sour to sweetness, bound up
The bleeding white of junction with broad strips
Of working flannel-shirt and belly-bands
To join the two in union. For a time
After the wound healed the sweetness held,
The balance tilted towards an old delight.

But in the time that I remember him
(His wife had long since died, I never saw her)
The sour half took over. Every single apple
Grew — across twenty Augusts — bitter as wormwood.
He'd sit under the box tree, his pink gums
(Between the white moustache and goatee beard)
Grinding thin slices that his jack-knife cut,
Sucking for sweetness vainly. It had gone,
Gone. I heard him mutter
Quiet Welsh oaths as he spat the gall-juice
Into the seeding onion-bed, watched him toss
The big core into the spreading nettles.

Cathedral Builders

They climbed on sketchy ladders towards God,
With winch and pulley hoisted hewn rock into heaven,
Inhabited sky with hammers, defied gravity,
Deified stone, took up God's house to meet Him,

And came down to their suppers and small beer;
Every night slept, lay with their smelly wives,
Quarrelled and cuffed the children, lied,
Spat, sang, were happy or unhappy,

And every day took to the ladders again;
Impeded the rights of way of another summer's
Swallows, grew greyer, shakier, became less inclined
To fix a neighbour's roof of a fine evening,

Saw naves sprout arches, clerestories soar,
Cursed the loud fancy glaziers for their luck,

Somehow escaped the plague, got rheumatism,
Decided it was time to give it up,

To leave the spire to others; stood in the crowd
Well back from the vestments at the consecration,
Envied the fat bishop his warm boots,
Cocked up a squint eye and said, 'I bloody did that'.

The Key

Its teeth worked doubtfully
At the worn wards of the lock,
Argued half-heartedly
With the lock's fixed dotage.
Between them they deferred decision.
One would persist, the other
Not relent. That lock and key
Were old when Linus Yale
Himself was born. Theirs
Was an ageless argument.

The key was as long as my hand,
The ring of it the size
Of a girl's bangle. The bit
Was inches square. A grandiose key
Fit for a castle, yet our terraced
House was two rooms up, two down;
Flung there by sullen pit-owners
In a spasm of petulance, discovering
That colliers could not live
On the bare Welsh mountain:

Like any other house in the domino
Row, except that our door
Was nearly always on the latch.
Most people just walked in, with
'Anybody home?' in greeting
To the kitchen. This room
Saw paths of generations cross;
This was the place to which we all came
Back to talk by the oven, on the white
Bench. This was the home patch.

And so, if we went out, we hid
The key — though the whole village
Knew where it was — under a stone
By the front door. We lifted up
The stone, deposited the key
Neatly into its own shape
In the damp earth. There, with liquid
Metal, we could have cast,
Using that master mould,
Another key, had we had need of it.

Sometimes we'd dip a sea-gull's
Feather in oil, corkscrew it
Far into the keyhole to ease
The acrimony there. The feather, askew
In the lock, would spray black
Droplets of oil on the threshold
And dandruff of feather-barb.
The deep armoreal stiffness, tensed
Against us, stayed. We'd put away
The oil, scrub down the front step.

The others have gone for the long
Night away. The evidence of grass
Re-growing insists on it. This time
I come back to dispose of what there is.
The knack's still with me. I plunge home
The key's great stem, insinuate
Something that was myself between
The two old litigants. The key
Engages and the bolt gives to me
Some walls enclosing furniture.

In September

Again the golden month, still
Favourite, is renewed;
Once more I'd wind it in a ring
About your finger, pledge myself
Again, my love, my shelter,
My good roof over me,
My strong wall against winter.

Be bread upon my table still
And red wine in my glass; be fire
Upon my hearth. Continue,
My true storm door, continue
To be sweet lock to my key;
Be wife to me, remain
The soft silk on my bed.

Be morning to my pillow,
Multiply my joy. Be my rare coin
For counting, my luck, my
Granary, my promising fair
Sky, my star, the meaning
Of my journey. Be, this year too,
My twelve months long desire.

Design for a Quilt

First let there be a tree, roots taking ground
In bleached and soft blue fabric.
Into the well-aired sky, branches extend
Only to bend away from the turned-back
Edge of linen where day's horizons end;

Branches symmetrical, not over-flaunting
Their leaves (let ordinary swansdown
Be their lining), which in the summertime
Will lie lightly upon her, the girl
This quilt's for, this object of designing;

But such, too, when deep frosts veneer
Or winds prise at the slates above her,
Or snows lie in the yard in a black sulk,
That the embroidered cover, couched
And applied with pennants of green silk,

Will still be warm enough that should she stir
To draw a further foliage about her
The encouraged shoots will quicken
And, at her breathing, midnight's spring
Can know new season as they thicken.

Feather-stitch on every bough
A bird, one neat French-knot its eye,
To sing a silent night-long lullaby
And not disturb her or disbud her.
See that the entwining motives run

In and about themselves to bring
To bed the sheens and mossy lawns of Eden;
For I would have a perfect thing
To echo if not equal Paradise
As garden for her true temptation:

So that in future times, recalling
The pleasures of past falling, she'll bequeath it
To one or other of the line,
Bearing her name or mine,
With luck I'll help her make beneath it.

Design for a Tomb

Dwell in this stone who once was tenant of flesh.
Alas, lady, the phantasmagoria is over,
Your smile must come to terms with dark for ever.

Carved emblems, puff-cheeked cherubs and full vines,
Buoy up your white memorial in the chapel,
Weightlessly over you who welcomed a little weight.

Lie unprotesting who often lay in the dark,
Once trembling switchback lady keep your stillness
Lest marble crack, ornate devices tumble.

Old melodies were loth to leave your limbs,
Love's deft reluctances where many murmured delight
Lost all their gay glissandi, grew thin and spare

Between a few faint notes. Your bright fever
Turned towards cold, echoed remembered sweets.
Those who for years easily climbed to your casement

Left by the bare front hall. Lust grown respectable
Waltzed slow knight's moves under the portico,
Crabbed in a black gown. You were carried out

Feet first, on your back, still, over the broad chequers.
So set up slender piers, maidenhair stone
Like green fern springing again between ivory oaks,

The four main pillars to your canopy;
And underneath it, up near the cornices,
Let in small fenestrations to catch the light.

It still chinks, spy-holing the bent laurel
With worn footholds outside your bedroom window
Through which you'd hear an early gardener's hoe

Chivvy the small weeds on the gravel path
Only to turn dazedly back into your lover's arms,
Fumblingly to doze, calling the morning false.

Lady-lust so arrayed in ornamental bed,
Baring your teeth for the first apple of heaven,
Juices and sap still run. Sleep, well-remembered.

The Gift

From where, from whom? Why ask, in torment
All life long when, while we live, we live in it?
As pointless to ask for truth in epiphanies
That throb in the fire, rustle, then fall into ash;
Or why stars are not black in a white firmament.
Enough that it was given, green, as of right, when,
Equally possible, nothing might ever have been.

JOYCE HERBERT
Dossers at the Imperial War Museum

A place devoted to death. At noon, when I came out, the sun
struck at my eyes. I'd been trying to hear Minnenwerfers,
catch the flare of a Verey light, the thud of a phosgene shell.

Across one wall a blinded daisychain of men went clambering
like stricken insects waving feeble antennae. Eyes burnt out,
they clutched the jacket of the man in front:

this neat clean dugout never knew them, neither did
the model soldier standing at the door, his webbing blancoed,
boots bright, puttees perfect, head high.
A general's delight.

There were photographs of running figures wavering,
lurching, buckling at the knees. There were humped heaps
fallen, stranded like fish on a desolate beach.

Sunshine showered sparks, drenched the steps.
I could not see, shaded my eyes.
They were all out there. Some tide of war had washed them
down the steps from Bapaume or the Somme,
rolled in cocoons of blankets, sprawled on their backs, knees up,
spilled on the shaven grass:
prone near the flowerbeds they slept like stones,
jaws dropped, mittened fingers clutching.
Far under bushes I could see them
in attitudes of death,
rolled in their plastic bags waiting for something to happen.

The Irish Scullery Maid

I smell dry snuffy turf smoke clouding the cottages
on Sunday. I hear the massed patter of little hooves,
all the asscarts squeaking and grumbling,
people perched, old sacks in the mist.
A soft Meath morning.

Rumble of it, thousands of little hooves
totter trotting,
ash-plants burning the grey backs.

Light thickening,
blurred wobbling armies of asscarts
blown to the four winds,
massed asses for Mass in Meath,
I wish I was bunched on the edge of our cart,
soaked with dew from the dark hedges,
I wish I was feeling the stones grinding my knees,
half asleep watching the old sogarth

clambering about the Altar,
and the damp rising like steam
off the backs of the people.
Anywhere but walking here before dawn.
I must walk and not stop walking.

The tongues of Meath
flail the seas.
The growth in my body
swings like a bell
when I move.
It pulls at my flesh
when I walk.
It burned in the hay
with the sweetness of fire.
The power of it roared into me.

There were dry stalks in my hair,
my shoulders on the hard field.

Her Ladyship wants to send me across the water,
home to the mouths of Meath,
the wrath of my father and mother,
the sly profiles of the men,
the heels of the children.
But I will sink with the weight of it
under the long waves.
Where the cliffs are highest by the lighthouse
I shall fall to the foam
like the piece of dung that I am.

November is hard.
Ice in my basin was thick this morning,
there was ice in the wheel-ruts.
I came between dark woods darker than the way,
when all the house was sleeping.
Bedded in stone the household dwindles from me.
Here's the laundry house, the lodge, the locked lodge gates.
But I'll use the gap in the wall where the ivy is thick
which I used when I went to my love.

Already I hear the low snarl of the sea.

The clifftop is cold.
It freezes me with its dislike.
The thing inside me is a frozen core,
it drags me down to the hard field,
where dead old grass stalks wait for the sun.
It will not mould itself to my bones, become
a permanent pressure, a mere nuisance.
No such luck. March is when it will yell itself out of me.

Ladyship's written to the priest.
He will knock our door with his blackthorn.

Because of the slope just here
you can't see the edge.

The sea is loud,
my skull is a shell for it.

Oh, my God, I promise
never to offend Thee again,
and carefully to avoid the occasion of sin. Amen.

Note: On the 8th Nov. 1895 the above took place at Monknash,
South Glamorgan.

DANNIE ABSE
Return to Cardiff

'Hometown'; well, most admit an affection for a city:
grey, tangled streets I cycled on to school, my first cigarette
in the back lane, and, fool, my first botched love affair.
First everything. Faded torments; self-indulgent pity.

The journey to Cardiff seemed less a return than a raid
on mislaid identities. Of course the whole locus smaller:
the mile-wide Taff now a stream, the castle not as in some black,
gothic dream, but a decent sprawl, a joker's toy façade.

Unfocused voices in the wind, associations, clues,
odds and ends, fringes caught, as when, after the doctor quit,

a door opened and I glimpsed the white, enormous face
of my grandfather, suddenly aghast with certain news.

Unable to define anything I can hardly speak,
and still I love the place for what I wanted it to be
as much as for what it unashamedly is
now for me, a city of strangers, alien and bleak.

Unable to communicate I'm easily betrayed,
uneasily diverted by mere sense reflections
like those anchored waterscapes that wander, alter, in the Taff,
hour by hour, as light slants down a different shade.

Illusory, too, that lost dark playground after rain,
the noise of trams, gunshots in what they once called Tiger Bay.
Only real this smell of ripe, damp earth when the sun comes out;
a mixture of pungencies, half exquisite and half plain.

No sooner than I'd arrived the other Cardiff had gone,
smoke in the memory, these but tinned resemblances,
where the boy I was not and the man I am not
met, hesitated, left double footsteps, then walked on.

Hunt the Thimble

Hush now. You cannot describe it.

Is it like heavy rain falling,
and lights going on, across the fields,
in the new housing estate?

Cold, cold. Too domestic, too
temperate, too devoid of history.

Is it like a dark windowed street at night,
the houses uncurtained, the street deserted?

Colder. You are getting colder,
and too romantic, too dream-like.
You cannot describe it.

The brooding darkness then,
that breeds inside a cathedral
of a provincial town in Spain?

In Spain, also, but not Spanish.
In England, if you like, but not English.
It remains, even when obscure, perpetually.
Aged, but ageless, you cannot describe it.
No, you are cold, altogether too cold.

Aha — the blue sky over Ampourias,
the blue sky over Lancashire for that matter ...

You cannot describe it.

... obscured by clouds?
I must know what you mean.

Hush, hush.

Like those old men in hospital dying,
who, unaware strangers stand around their bed,
stare obscurely, for a long moment,
at one of their own hands raised —
which perhaps is bigger than the moon again —
and then, drowsy, wandering, shout out, 'Mama'.

Is it like that? Or hours after that even:
the darkness inside a dead man's mouth?

No, no, I have told you:
you are cold, and you cannot describe it.

Photograph and White Tulips

A little nearer please. And a little nearer
we move to the window, to the polished table.
Objects become professional: mannequins
preening themselves before an audience. Only
the tulips, self-absorbed, ignore the camera.

All photographs flatter us if we wait
long enough. So we awkwardly Smile please
while long-necked tulips, sinuous out of the vase,

droop over the polished table. They're entranced
by their own puffed and smudged reflections.

Hold it! Click. Once more! And we smile again
at one who'll be irrevocably absent.
Quick. Be quick! the tulips, like swans, will dip
their heads deep into the polished table
frightening us. Thank you. And we turn thinking,

What a fuss! Yet decades later, dice thrown,
we'll hold it, thank you, this fable of gone
youth (was that us?) and we shall smile please
and come a little nearer to the impetuous
once-upon-a-time that can never be twice.

(Never never be twice!) Yet we'll always recall
how white tulips, quick quick, changed into swans
enthralled, drinking from a polished table.
As for those white petals, they'll never fall
in that little black coffin now carrying us.

Pathology of Colours

I know the colour rose, and it is lovely,
but not when it ripens in a tumour;
and healing greens, leaves and grass, so springlike,
in limbs that fester are not springlike.

I have seen red-blue tinged with hirsute mauve
in the plum-skin face of a suicide.
I have seen white, china white almost, stare
from behind the smashed windscreen of a car.

And the criminal, multi-coloured flash
of an H-bomb is no more beautiful
than an autopsy when the belly's opened —
to show cathedral windows never opened.

So in the simple blessing of a rainbow,
in the bevelled edge of a sunlit mirror,
I have seen, visible, Death's artifact
like a soldier's ribbon on a tunic tacked.

In the theatre
(A true incident)

'Only a local anaesthetic was given because of the blood
pressure problem. The patient, thus, was fully awake through-
out the operation. But in those days — in 1938, in Cardiff,
when I was Lambert Rogers' dresser — they could not locate
a brain tumour with precision. Too much normal brain tissue
was destroyed as the surgeon crudely searched for it, before
he felt the resistance of it ... all somewhat hit and miss. One
operation I shall never forget ....' (Dr Wilfred Abse)

Sister saying — 'Soon you'll be back in the ward,'
sister thinking — 'Only two more on the list,'
the patient saying — 'Thank you, I feel fine';
small voices, small lies, nothing untoward,
though, soon, he would blink again and again
because of the fingers of Lambert Rogers,
rash as a blind man's, inside his soft brain.

If items of horror can make a man laugh
then laugh at this: one hour later, the growth
still undiscovered, ticking its own wild time;
more brain mashed because of the probe's braille path;
Lambert Rogers desperate, fingering still;
his dresser thinking, 'Christ! Two more on the list,
a cisternal puncture and a neural cyst.'

Then, suddenly, the cracked record in the brain,
a ventriloquist voice that cried, 'You sod,
leave my soul alone, leave my soul alone,' —
the patient's dummy lips moving to that refrain,
the patient's eyes too wide. And, shocked,
Lambert Rogers drawing out the probe
with nurses, students, sister, petrified.

'Leave my soul alone, leave my soul alone,'
that voice so arctic and that cry so odd
had nowhere else to go — till the antique
gramophone wound down and the words began
to blur and slow, '... leave ... my ... soul ... alone ...'
to cease at last when something other died.
And silence matched the silence under snow.

Case History

'Most Welshmen are worthless,
an inferior breed, doctor.'
He did not know I was Welsh.
Then he praised the architects
of the German death-camps —
did not know I was a Jew.
He called liberals, 'White blacks',
and continued to invent curses.

When I palpated his liver
I felt the soft liver of Goering;
when I lifted my stethoscope
I heard the heartbeats of Himmler;
when I read his encephalograph
I thought, *'Sieg heil, mein Führer.'*

In the clinic's dispensary
red berry of black bryony,
cowbane, deadly nightshade, deathcap.
Yet I prescribed for him
as if he were my brother.

Later that night I must have slept
on my arm: momentarily
my right hand lost its cunning.

Welsh Valley Cinema, 1930s

In The Palace of the slums,
from the Saturday night pit,
from an unseen shaft of darkness
I remember it: how, first, a sound
took wing grandly; then the thrill
of a fairground sight — it rose,
lordly stout thing, boasting
a carnival of gaudy-bright,
changing colours while wheezing out
swelling rhonchi of musical asthma.

I hear it still, played with panache
by renowned gent, Cathedral Jones,

'When the Broadway Baby Says Goodnight
It's Early in the Morning' — then he and it
sank to disappear, a dream underground.

Later, those, downstairs, gobbing silicosis
(shoeless feet on the mecca carpet),
observed a miracle — the girl next door,
a poor ragged Goldilocks,
dab away her glycerine tears
to kiss cuff-linked Cary Grant
under an elegance of chandeliers.
(No flies on Cary. No holes in *his* socks.)

And still the Woodbine smoke swirled on
in the opium beam of the operator's box
till THE END — of course, upbeat.
Then from The Palace, the damned Fall,
the glum, too silent trooping out
into the trauma of paradox:
the familiar malice of the dreary,
unemployed, gas-lamped street
and the striking of the small Town's clocks.

Thankyou Note

for the unbidden swish of morning curtains
you opened wide — letting sleep-baiting shafts
of sunlight enter to lie down by my side;
for adagio afternoons when you did the punting
(my toiling eyes researched the shifting miles of sky);
for back-garden evenings when you chopped the wood
and I, incomparably, did the grunting;
(a man too good for this world of snarling
is no good for his wife — truth's the safest lie);

for applauding my poetry, O most perceptive spouse;
for the improbable and lunatic, my darling;
for amorous amnesties after rancorous rows
like the sweet-nothing whisperings of a leafy park
after the blatant noise of a city street
(exit booming cannons, enter peaceful ploughs);
for kindnesses the blind side of my night-moods;
for lamps you brought in to devour the dark.

RAYMOND GARLICK
Dylan Thomas at Tenby

Into the pause, while peppermints were passed
after the strong piano's breathless Brahms,
he walked and took his place, sat down and cast

(expressionless of face) an eye abroad,
moving the carafe with a marked distaste.
His fame proclaimed, he looked politely bored

and crossed his legs and lit a cigarette,
screwing his eyes up at the smart of smoke.
So all was done and said. The scene was set

for speech, and nervously he stirred and spoke —
shuffling the pack of papers on his knee,
at random drew one, stared at it and woke

into awareness. Now the sleeping town
under the wood of Wales sat up and sang,
rose from its river bed and eiderdown

of ducks, strode heron-stilted through the dark
and rode white horses, nightmares from the sea,
across a *cantref* to this bay's bright arc

and the Noah of a poet calling there
to his creatures to come. Two by two, word
by word they marched from his mouth, pair by pair

to the beat of the drum of his tongue
and the trumpet of his lips. In the ships
of his speech the saga sailed and was sung.

And Tenby, their harbour, attended.
It was October, the month of birthdays.
The saga was nearly ended.

Consider Kyffin

Consider Kyffin, now — as Welsh
a word-spinner as you could wish,
who wove in both tongues, using yours

before you some four hundred years;
John Davies out of Hereford,
Holland of Denbigh — men who fired
their flintlocks through the border wall
loaded with English words as well.
Remember Lloyds and Llwyds, Vaughans,
who opened with their quills both veins
of language, giving life to myth —
the forked tongue in the dragon's mouth.
The others, too, who went astray
down some bypath of history —
their Welsh but not their Welshness lost:
in all, upon the muse's list
a hundred names — your pedigree,
your greener branches of the tree.

In silted bays of old bookshops —
shelved and becalmed like ancient ships
in saffron havens, I have rocked
their boats, long run aground and wrecked;
eased dusty covers open, looked,
clambered inside entranced, unlocked
each bulkhead page from stern to beak
and in the cabin of his book
come on the poet at his ease.
Some — seamen, scribbling in the haze
of voyages to where Wales joins
the world's end: Samwell, Poet Jones.
Others — upcountry parsons, squires,
hotblood students in Oxford squares,
curates penning the Poems of Hughes —
by candlelight in a creaking house
under the wheeling universe
cutting and polishing a verse.

They are the root from which you stem —
but you have never heard of them.

Note on the Iliad

Why are epics
Always about
The anti-life
Of a noble lout?

I sing Lely
Who burnt no tower
But brought the sea-floor
Into flower.

Imagine it —
The moment when
Out of the
Architectured fen

The polder surfaced
Sleek as a whale
And still awash.
Then the last veil

Of standing water
Slides away.
Glistening land
Like a wet tray

Serves up its past,
Wreck upon wreck
Glazed in the sand
Of this smooth deck:

Like Ararat,
The antique shores
Ride up again
Ready for Noahs.

Now wheat ripples
Where schooner and barque
Thrashed down the waters
To ultimate dark —

Avenued Holland
Waves over plains
Which twenty years back
Rocked fishing-seines.

Hard to imagine
The North Sea floor
Was where we picnic —
And even more

To imagine this:
A people at grips
With genesis
Not apocalypse.

Behind the Headlines

Herodotus, while gossiping
With some old clergymen who ran
The Memphis temple, heard from them
It was to Egypt Paris came
With stolen Helen. They were wrecked
    By the salt-pans, lived there for a while
    Alongside the Canopic Nile.

(Canopic and the salt-pans seem
Authentic details.) Then the Greeks
Sent messengers to Troy and asked
For Helen and their money back.
The Trojans hadn't got them, but
    Generals are much inclined to fight
    The wrong battle on the wrong site.

And so the ten years' war ensued:
The thousand ships took to the sea,
Then all that wooden horse affair,
And Troy at last put to the flames:
All a mistake. Herodotus,
    Having sorted out this mystery,
    Continued researching history.

The Heiress

With glittering fingers, diamond brooch,
A rope of pearls, each tinted perfect curl,
She told the story he'd already heard
From others. A typical Dutch girl,
Shy, sedate, demure, honouring Vader
And Moeder, and Queen Wilhelmina too;
    Doing her homework and walking the dog,
    Going each sabbath to the synagogue.

At first the war did not have much effect
In pink brick, innocent suburban streets:
It was a Party Occupation, not
Street to street fighting, and bourgeois retreats
Were inwards. Then posters went up and said
All Jewish families should gather at
  The railway station at a given hour.
  Good citizens, used to a good State's power

Used always for the good of citizens,
They gathered quietly at the stated time
In whispering hundreds and got on the train.
But just as Miriam was going to climb
Aboard after her parents, she was swept
By terrible foreboding. She stepped down
  Into the crowd unnoticed, slipping back
  Into the bushes by the railway track.

Appalled at what she had done, she watched
The last of the crowd get on, and saw
At a window her parents' agonized
Faces looking for her. Then the last door
Was slammed. Slowly the train began to move
Away from the station towards the east.
  Soon the long platform was silent and bare
  Except for the German guards smiling there.

No one ever returned. Neighbours hid her
Through the long, anguished years that were to come.
Even of her extended family
No single one survived. And so the sum
Of everything, years after, came to her.
But Miriam, he reasoned, You chose life.
  She shrugged her shoulders, bent her coiffured head,
  And wept and wept, would not be comforted.

MERCER SIMPSON
Homo Erectus, Cerne Abbas

Think of your age, old man:
keeping anything up too long
can lead to problems:

exhaustion, frustration,
brandishing that phallic club,
waiting for something exciting
or for someone that, like Godot,
never comes; that woman, now,
alleged to have been on your left hand,
who stood you up a thousand years ago,
she's invisible because she's been
put out to grass, even though
she must have got you going
at the beginning,
idol with feet of chalk
instead of clay, standing
two thousand years, the longest
erection in history.
On the smooth green curve
of downland above your head
the villagers would celebrate
the rites of May, young men
and virgins garlanded
in a deflorescent
expectancy; but little
satisfaction you must have got
out of it, but that they kept
your white lines sharp and clean,
nearly all flesh being grass
but memory evergreen.

JOHN TRIPP
The Last at Lucy's

On Fridays we would gather at Lucy's,
He squatting like a Buddha well fed
While my eye kept shifting from poetry
To a poetess I wanted in bed.

Cleverness flowed. They would carve up
Some boy with a questing nerve
Who was baffled by the hothouse breeders
All tingling with cerebral verve.

'What do *you* think, Fudge?
Did you like it, Climp? How about you, Slob?
Miss Bunbum, what's your view?'
I saw the meat of the bone, the premature death of a cub.

Tea-cups clinked, marzipan offered round
As the poets stabbed absent friends.
What was happening was most important,
A small arrow to significant trends.

They would tack back and forth on a single line
And the mumbo-jumbo would spill;
I thought of Thomas and poor Hart Crane
Who would be ripe here for the kill.

Now it is over, and Lucy himself
Saw one day through the damage done;
The egos, they came and went,
Banging their own tin drum.

There in Chelsea the Muse was kept
Locked in the cold deep-freeze.
I never slept with the nice poetess,
With an icicle she found her ease.

Note: A group of poets used to meet in Edward Lucie-Smith's
London home during the 1960s. (Ed.)

Caroline Street, Cardiff

Curry spice in the air,
the smell of burnt paratha.
You'd have thought you were in Bombay.

Shops full of rubber goods:
huge dusty cartons of Durex,
enough for a cavalry charge on Maidenhead.

The second-hand bookcrap:
pulp crime and pulp sex,
hot porno for the sly ferrets
loitering in trilbies and mackintoshes;

the odd book of poems
lying there like a virgin in a brothel.

And the restaurant where we ate each other's eyes
over pie and chips —
the authentic thing, the slow slide into love.
We felt so good,
that place of hissing chip vats and crusted ketchup bottles
could have been the Savoy Grill.

Armistice Day '77, Honiton

The two minutes' silence was cut to one
that November day; it was a busy world.
By chance, on my way to a gig,
I walked into a ceremony of six
in the rain: crosses in a ring, and the poppies soaked.

Down two sides of the slab were names
linked to this piece of England — the sound
of country stock grown old in duty
and the acceptance of pointless loss.
Names going back to Minden and before.

(Were these the only ones left
to remember their dead?
Already sixty seconds were lopped
off any dignity. Would their children
forget, as I had forgotten?)

No more came. On some other day
I might have felt an interloper
marring their ritual. At eleven o'clock
the men took off their hats
and we all bowed our heads.

A minute in the rain in a country town
may whisper the whole grief of history.
Picture a knot of seven around that block,
the red wet poppies, and for just a moment
a complete and utter silence in the world.

Ploughman

'You may not get a chance
to see this again,' the correspondent
from Power Farming said to me.

Near Builth I watched him
slowly carve up a plot
in neat straight grooves, doing
a precision high-cut run
with the polished furrow slices
gleaming like metal.
He turned through an exact angle
of a hundred-and-thirty degrees
without breaking, and packing firm
against the previous slice.
It was the true straightness
of the lines you had to see,
as if he steered along white paint.

The shires stopped on a tuppence
when he yelled Whoa!
They stopped with one foot in the air
and put it back, not forward.
He fussed and tuned his ship
when he felt a slight change
of texture, or the horses leaned
into a breeze. He did an acre
a day, walking ten miles
behind the big patient team.
A really bad error was visible
in soil or crop for a year.
His craft seemed timeless, and beautiful.

He was one of the last
of his skill. I'm glad I saw it
before his plough went to a museum.

Twilight in the Library

I have not come within their frozen
North, but we all go there
sometime. The entry visa

is age and complete silence
broken only by pages turning.
On a wall is a fitting print
of old people drowsy in Salem.
It takes months of visits, scanning
curled copies of *Punch*
or *Harper's Bazaar*, to reserve your seat.

I offer the old men tobacco
for a roll; they accept me tardily
into the room. They take turns
to keep the tiers of racks tidy
and journals in their proper slots.
                                                  They trail
bleak lifetimes behind them ...
and cough and cough. The Elder
has a red nose and silver stubble,
his magnifier races across *The Times*
and *Guardian*. He is the group's
intellectual, full of useless facts,
making notes in a secret pad
and scribbling faster as closing-time comes.

Rain drips down the sooted panes.
The Elder wheezes over a magazine
while his cronies grunt and sleep, creaking
into December, warming themselves
against hot pipes, propped at the long tables.

There is a sense of all the days ending,
a reluctance to face the night
as the lights come on in the precinct
and a keeper points to the clock.

Connection in Bridgend

In the bus café, drinking tea, I watch
nothing happening in Bridgend.
I mean, there is rain, some shoppers
under canopies, tyres sloshing them
from the gutters. Otherwise not much.

(Do those Pakistanis feel the cold?
What are they doing in Bridgend?
How did they land here, and those lost
Sikhs and Chinamen?
I am sorry for them, they look bereft.)

In the café a young mother is being given
stick by her two boys. They want Coke
and her baby cries for no reason
unless he's seen enough of Bridgend.
I feel an odd kinship with him.

At last my bacon sandwich is done;
it was something to look forward to,
slicing a minute's delight into the murk.
Balancing the plate, I hold the sad babe
while his mother fetches the Coke.

Then a one-armed paperseller comes in
with a strip of frayed ribbons on his coat.
He wants to tell me his story,
so I listen while the baby sobs
and his brothers suck straws.

An hour ago, I was alone; now
there are six. Even the café-owner
squeezes out a smile. We are in it
together, until the last buses go out.
One by one they leave the bays.

Father

If you should come to our silent
bungalow, he will either be potting
in the greenhouse, or mending something.
A clock, for instance. Our place
is full of timepieces, resurrected
from scrap. These tick and chime
all night, keeping guests awake.
I see his white head bend
over tomato plants, his fingers pick
with a penknife at a flywheel
in the littered shed. Then later

he cooks for us, a folded Cornish
pasty, seeping nourishment.
He is supreme at baking cake.

There were dark calamitous months
he lived through, the widower's
grieved adjustment to emptiness
after forty years. 'I preferred
the Somme,' he said to me.
She was as close to his side
as a woman could be, an exact
counterpart of a true maker,
destroying nothing. And now
in his late evening I see
all that I had missed before:
the calm, the patience, the kindness,
the country simplicity he wears,
that I will not inherit.

CHRISTINE FURNIVAL
Rhiannon

How welcome it is, how sweet that the old stories do not always
    tell
of smoking citadels and beauty that drove men mad,
of big-headed, dirty old gods (and goddesses); of dispiriting
    visits to hell
and those entire sewer-networks of curses where pacific citizens
    end up dead;
yes, in the catastrophic hour, how extremely refreshing and good

it is to encounter those rare, important — even royal — top
    persons
who are more intent on living than making ready to die;
who speak some funny lines and act with individual wisdom,
and are so endearing that we feel a captivated envy
of the ease they bring to being beautiful and good. — Rhiannon

was such a lady, daughter of Hefeydd the Old — who herself aged
slowly, with strong, comely grace — right from the moment

she unveiled herself to Pwyll, Prince of Dyfed
to those days when, widowed and re-married,
she rose, with a smile, to homelessness and some malign
   enchantments.

She was witty & forthright — as when she told her diffident
   young suitor
she loved only him — an idiot who should have spoken his
   mind before;
forbearing too, at times, — a stoic who could say 'poor creatures'
to those who perjured truth to make her suffer.
Light-hearted common-sense she brought to being out of work
   and poor.

In fact, she found it hard to put a foot wrong —
yet dodged self-righteousness; was earthy, gay and real;
took in her generous stride a life clear and resilient as bird-song
as, bedded, widowed and beggared in wet Wales
she always soldiered on.

TONY CONRAN
Elegy for the Welsh Dead, in the Falkland Islands, 1982

> Gwŷr a aeth Gatraeth oedd ffraeth eu llu.
> Glasfedd eu hancwyn, a gwenwyn fu.
>   — *Y Gododdin* (6th century)

> (Men went to Catraeth, keen was their company.
> They were fed on fresh mead, and it proved poison.)

Men went to Catraeth. The luxury liner
For three weeks feasted them.
They remembered easy ovations,
Our boys, splendid in courage.
For three weeks the albatross roads,
Passwords of dolphin and petrel,
Practised their obedience
Where the killer whales gathered,
Where the monotonous seas yelped.
Though they went to church with their standards
Raw death has them garnished.

Men went to Catraeth. The Malvinas
Of their destiny greeted them strangely,
Instead of affection there was coldness,
Splintering iron and the icy sea,
Mud and the wind's malevolent satire.
They stood nonplussed in the bomb's indictment.

Malcolm Wigley of Connah's Quay. Did his helm
Ride high in the war-line?
Did he drink enough mead for that journey?
The desolated shores of Tegeingl,
Did they pig this steel that destroyed him?
The Dee runs silent beside empty foundries.
The way of the wind and the rain is adamant.

Clifford Elley of Pontypridd. Doubtless he feasted.
He went to Catraeth with a bold heart.
He was used to valleys. The shadow held him.
The staff and the fasces of tribunes betrayed him.
With the oil of our virtue we have anointed
His head, in the presence of foes.

Phillip Sweet of Cwmbach. Was he shy before girls?
He exposes himself now to the hags, the glance
Of the loose-fleshed whores, the deaths
That congregate like gulls on garbage.
His sword flashed in the wastes of nightmare.

Russell Carlisle of Rhuthun. Men of the North
Mourn Rheged's son in the castellated vale.
His nodding charger neighed for the battle.
Uplifted hooves pawed at the lightning.
Now he lies down. Under the air he is dead.

Men went to Catraeth. Of the forty-three
Certainly Tony Jones of Carmarthen was brave.
What did it matter, steel in the heart?
Shrapnel is faithful now. His shroud is frost.

With the dawn men went. Those forty-three,
Gentlemen all, from the streets and byways of Wales,
Dragons of Aberdare, Denbigh and Neath —
Figment of empire, whore's honour, held them.
Forty-three at Catraeth died for our dregs.

Spirit Level
(for George and Sue, in New Guinea)

An odd gift, certainly. One
Would have to be hard up
To give such a thing for a wedding.
A plate or a cup

Or Eighteenth Century pot —
Rustic, of course,
Embellished with two seated lovers
And a grazing horse;

Or else a spied treasure of bronze
From Samarkand —
A perfectionist's quodlibet
From a shop on the Strand —

Ah, these would be elegant gifts,
And surely would raise
The naked Papuans to envy
The White Man's ways.

I wish I had thought of them sooner,
Or luck had slunk
To the wellnigh miraculous gift
In a shopful of junk.

But my eye has domiciled with this
Uncompromising wood,
Its brass fittings inelegant,
Its proportions crude.

Drab product of a technology
That has left it behind,
A tool mass-produced without passion
Of body or mind ...

But through its window the small, oblong
Bubble of oil
— Wherever you are, on English
Or New Guinean soil —

Still keeps its strange relationship
To the round earth
And points to the perfect tangent
Of its spheroid girth.

The awe-inspiring simplicity
Of that design
Makes irrelevant lack of grace
And brutal line.

Such is my emblem for how I honour you,
For what I give
Comes from the responding eye
Where all truths live.

I pray for you through this emblem
That each of you in each,
The straight wood, the bubble of oil,
True centre reach,

And right-angled with the world,
Hold its full sphere
With the delicate poise
Of the hoof of a deer.

Thirteen Ways of Looking at a Hoover
(for Barbara Zanditon)

i
The party suddenly condensed
To the four of us —
Him, and him and her, and me.

I have never seen anger so elegant!
He checkmates them
Lifting their legs
To hoover, ruthlessly, their chair-space.

ii
A hoover is like a camel —
It humps itself with provender
And can be trained to spit.

iii
One would hardly believe
That even four humans and two cats
Gave so much skin.

Yet, once a week,
The bloated paper intestine of this beast
Has to be emptied of our bits of death.

iv
The difficult slow ease of scything hay —
It is comparable
To her adroitness with its wheels and flex.

v
After many days of toothache
To be grateful for the amnesia
Of a dentist's chair.

And after the long chaos of builders,
Carpenters, electricians,
Destroyers of plaster —

To be sensuously grateful
For the din of a hoover.

vi
In their iron age
The antique hoovers
— All pistons and steel tubes and levers —
In our square-carpeted drawing-rooms
Did not disguise their alienation.

I once turned a corner in Liverpool
And saw, disappearing down a side-street,
A vast, black-leaded steam locomotive,
O-four-O, colossal amid cars.

The antique hoovers, one felt,
Were de-railed like that.

vii
Hoovers would like to be precise.
Their robot souls yearn for clearances

Plus or minus a thousandth of an inch.
Always, by wobble or pile or buffer,
They are betrayed. Your average yard-brush
Is more of a precision instrument!

viii
The soul of a hoover —
Is it the empty bag
That nothingness blows out like a sail?
Or is it the paradoxical geometry
Of the twisting belt, that burns
Sourly at the ingestion of a tack?

ix
There is a sub-culture of hoovers.
Hoovermen with wiry, terrier moustaches
Poke their heads from dusty limousines
To stop you in the road —

'That new belt I put in —
Has it remedied the fault?
Shall I come to see it?'

Their deft enquiries
Have strict authority over your thoughts.
The carry a king's seal, dispense his justice.

x
Its noise is more sensitive than you'd imagine.
It marks the difference between dusts.

xi
Most of us in a lifetime get to know
One, two, three hoovers. And that is enough.
We think we know the species.

But what of the professionals, the home-helps,
The Rent-a-maids from Hampstead?
Out of the hundreds of hoovers
Their fingers have caressed,
One, two, three stand out
Incomparable.

As they think of these
Majestic, suave, blond super-hoovers,
Their thighs grow supple with pride,
Their pupils take on the steady gleam
Of an enthusiast, they are fulfilled.

We don't know the half of what hoovers can do.

xii
On what authority you say it I don't know,
But you say, 'The hoover has no Muse'.
Yet from the murk and ashes of our common
Existence, the accumulating death
Of our lives together in this room,
The hoover creates darkness, order, love.
Its wake in the waves of a carpet
Makes lines of growth, furrows a field like a plough.

Could Erato of the laughing eyes, Urania,
Or Melpomene who bore to a slinky river-god
The enticing Sirens, half-girl, half-duck —

Could these *echt*-Muses have ordered it better?

xiii
It's a great virtue in hoovers
You can switch them off.

HARRY GUEST
Wales Re-visited

At home I have had to live as an alien.

The suspension-bridge, grey
rainbow spanning mud and tide,
landed me among the elms of autumn.

I was born on an October cliff
overlooking docks and islands.
Drizzle issued soft from the empty west.
My pram brushed thick hedges of fuchsia.

They took me young to learn a different language
far from those slopes red with bracken
where clearer water slides down levels of slate.

I remembered cairns where saints stood studying heaven,
dark galleries veined with gold and anthracite,
a saffron coastline littered with cowries and crab-shells,
those silhouetted castles, their high halls floored with grass.

Ships moor near a tower where lads play chess.
Shadows of heroes fight by the ruffled tarn.
A harper gives his message to the clouds.
I do not understand the words he sings.
I can no longer tell where I belong.

Not there where the legends have taken root,
not in my clanging birthplace, nor my adopted home,
not where I'm staying, nor where I want to be,
not where I travel to, nor the lands I've left,
not even there at last —
that green and windswept graveyard
where my forebears lie.

HERBERT WILLIAMS
The Old Tongue

We have lost the old tongue, and with it
The old ways too. To my father's
Parents it was one
With the gymanfa ganu, the rough
Shouts of seafarers, and the slow
Dawn of the universal light.
It was one with the home-made bread, the smell
Of cakes at missionary teas,
And the shadows falling
Remotely on the unattempted hills.

It is all lost, the tongue and the trade
In optimism. We have seen
Gethsemane in Swansea, marked
The massacre of innocents. The dawn

Was false and we invoke
A brotherhood of universal fear.
And the harbour makes
A doldrum of the summer afternoon.

Even the hills are diminished.
They are a gallon of petrol,
There and back. The old salts
Rot. And the bread
Is tasteless as a balance sheet.

Oh yes, there have been gains.
I merely state
That the language, for us,
Is part of the old, abandoned ways.

And when I hear it, regret
Disturbs me like a requiem.

SAM ADAMS
Rough Boys

Their father played the banjo,
Squatting on the doorstep in his pit clothes,
Dancing his steel-tipped boots
On a dirty patch of pavement.
And their brand of bullying was
    perversely merry
That to dream now of the rough and
    ragged brothers
Is not quite a nightmare.

They sold the banjo when the old man died:
A stone fell on him my father said.
Preserved in a state of innocence of the mine
By a small cleverness, I imagined a neat death,
Saw him carried whole up from the dark.
Years afterwards I heard the monstrous weight
The mountain shrugged on him.

Now in the bar those scab-kneed furies
Of my simple past are grown to
    quiet manhood,

and paradoxically shrunk.
The swaggering gait and tarzan cries
Are only in my memory.
They talk about their father, and their own
Daily intercourse with darkness,
Underground, held in that intimacy
Of coal like men in love,
I listen to the long and sad affair,
And feel, but fail to understand.

Gwbert: mackerel fishing

The small boat lurches, drifting,
A low sun flares from the sea.
We offer them senseless bait —
Draggled feathers, bits of plastic.

First one or two bend the rods,
Are hauled in and neatly detached,
Then their ecstasy of hunger
Explodes against the lines.

Kamikaze torpedoes,
They take anything, bare hooks,
Clamp themselves on the crude weights,
Missing the lure, are hooked through the eye.

The lines wound in through clouded glass
Heavy with struggling silver,
We tear them from the barbs;
Jaws dangle, cannibal bait.

Spurting excrement smears the deck,
Hands smoke-grey with fish slime;
In cold fever they thresh in blood,
Gills pulsing like butterflies.

Going home, we butcher them.
Gulls' chaos of wings and hideous cries
Pursue the boat like furies,
Diving for mackerel heads and guts.

Silvered by the water's skin,
White bird in ice, feathered fish,
Shark's ferocity of appetite,
They swallow whole the offal.

Perched cormorant in devil's pose,
Nazi badge at sunset,
Squirts a scornful comment
On the horde of scavengers.

Days later we still pick from our clothes
Fish scales like flakes of mica
Clinging with mackerel tenacity;
Months after the oily smell remains.

JON DRESSEL
Intercity, Swansea-London

The Sprinter from Carmarthen disgorges
its load, we spill across the platform
and feed into the leviathan, long and sleek,
that soon will move towards the end of Wales.

Neath, Port Talbot, Bridgend, Cardiff, Newport:
at first most accents, and many words, are Welsh,
but these diminish as we go, until we
become a British aggregation, and the cadences

of England abound in the cars. The tunnel
is negotiated, we ascend to Bristol,
take on more ballast, and power towards
the east. The hills of Wales lapse into memory,

green meadows stretch away on either side,
lush with grass and a different history.
The island is the same but the land grows larger,
holds more villages, towns and cities, stones.

Swindon and Reading overcome, we slow,
as if in reverence for the gravity of London.

We rattle through drab outskirts, study
backsides of flats, and squalid tower blocks

that are, and must be, homes. The sheer gray sprawl
of it seems less than human, makes me wince,
for all the Doctor Johnson in my soul.
The feeling does not last for long. It is

a yeoman reflex, old as towns, and has
truth in it, yet it does us wrong, denies
the ways that we stay small together, cut
our Londons down to size, whittle out our

nicks to live in, as we have to, as we can.
Brunel's great barn receives our load, doors open
and release us to enormous sound and motion,
I struggle, baggaged, out to London, glad.

Let's Hear It For Goliath

who never asked
to be born
either, let alone
grow nine feet

tall and wind
up a metaphor;
fat chance he
had of avoid-

ing the shove
from behind;
his old man
no doubt gave

him a sword
to teethe on,
and a scout
for the Philistine

host probably
had him under
contract by
the end of

junior high;
it was a fix;
and who wouldn't
have cursed

at the sight
of that arr-
ogant runt with
the sling, who,

for all his
psalms, would later
buy one wife
with a hundred

bloody pecker-
skins, and another
with a King's X
on Uriah; bah,

let's hear it
for Goliath, a big
boy who got
bad press but

who did his job,
absorbed a flukey
shot, and died
with a thud.

BRYN GRIFFITHS
The Master

You worked me well, Mr Thomas.
Duw, mun, all that writing
About an old nobody like me ...
Exposing me, Prytherch, like that.
Jiawl! Who would have believed it, mun —
Asking all those old questions all the time,
Ordering me about, just about,
And never believing anything I said ...

That day when you came down
From Moel y Llyn and asked me
(In Welsh, of course)
If I ever realised the drabness
Of my stark environment —
Whatever that meant —
And the meaning of my life ...
And you a vicar, too.

Well, now, Mr Thomas, I've never
Really given it much thought, you see —
I mean there's the farm to look after,
The milking, and the sheep to tend,
And one doesn't get much time
For other things. But I've fine company,
You know: Sian's a good dog,
A good friend.

You did push me a bit hard at times,
Mr Thomas, and tired me with talk,
But I don't really gob much, you know,
And I didn't care much for you saying
Of my 'half-witted grin'.
I'm not dull. I go to the eisteddfodau
And I know all about englynion —
And what more do I need than that?

You're in your world and I'm in mine.
I don't go to church, you see —
Chapel's good enough for me!
(And you making the village
Work to your words ....)
I mean, who are you to talk?
Up there, high and mighty in your vicarage,
Playing the lord in Eglwys Fach.

Dolphins

The shimmering sea is still —
till a detonation in the deeps
sends the gentle fury exploding

upwards, upwards, towards the bright
roof of the world where the dark
green of the world

pales into another sea
of incredible light:
the sky breaks, shatters, parts

under the soaring hurl of silver
weight that splits the waterface
with white spray:

a school of dolphin flashes
into sight ... And here we watch,
we shackled men,

while the dolphins wheel and spin
and march in foaming echelons
through the long hot day to weigh

our minds with millennial doubt
of man's ways — the lack of fluke
and fin to surge deep and swim.

Our ship drives on, a dust mote
on the waterclock, and now
the day dies to bring down night

in the swift tropic extinction
of light as the dolphins drift away,
leaving two alone to watch over us,

knifing through the night alongside,
scissoring endlessly, leap over leap,
in the green fire of phosphorescence

which breaks about our bow ...
For miles, long sea miles, they hurtle
alongside, their fixed grin of ages

seeming to pity us, and then
they wheel away in sudden flight —
their bulleting bodies gone into night!

SALLY ROBERTS JONES
Household Cavalry, Llanstephan
(for Dylan and Nesta)

We took the children down for an hour's outing,
Plenty of sun and sand and a good safe beach.
But there were the horses: perfect, bright shapes of wonder,
Tugging the stubborn grass with their vicious teeth.

Last night we had heard the music of their passage,
Drumming of hooves on the turf, the trumpeted air
Reeling at so much glory. Today we saw them
At ease in the picket lines on the littered Green.

Too much for the children; that majesty, beyond them,
Something to know in a later year. They turned,
Exhausted, to mine the sand, and build their castle,
A bulwark against the gentle tide's advance.

Soon, when their riders came, the horses altered;
No longer the distant princes, they plunged among us,
Raced in the shallow waves, set careless hoof marks
Flat on our broken fort, spurned shells and children.

Dangerous, yes; like lightning or flood or fire:
Something we could not contain, yet would not escape:
There, on the warm, safe sand, the horses of anger
Already rode down the children as they played.

Another Lazarus

At first, come back, I'd nothing else to do
But sit where the steady shadows of the vine
Kept me in shade, where waking in the heat
I saw my sisters sprawl across the step,
Mouths slack, limbs coarse, hair stringy with their sweat.

No sort of beauty: as we always were,
So were we now, when neither good nor bad
Were relevant; the miracle was past,
God's pity spent. Slowly I learnt to walk,
To speak, at last to move without command.

Standing in shade, I saw my sisters crouch
Whisper to whisper, saw their man of clay
Grow to my height, my colour — my despair:
Gently they breathed, with love, my life to him,
Living that he might die and they be saved.

I was my own; and passed, near Bethany,
Two sisters mourning at an empty grave.

GILLIAN CLARKE
Baby-Sitting

I am sitting in a strange room listening
For the wrong baby. I don't love
This baby. She is sleeping a snuffly
Roseate, bubbling sleep; she is fair;
She is a perfectly acceptable child.
I am afraid of her. If she wakes
She will hate me. She will shout
Her hot midnight rage, her nose
Will stream disgustingly and the perfume
Of her breath will fail to enchant me.

To her I will represent absolute
Abandonment. For her it will be worse
Than for the lover cold in lonely
Sheets; worse than for the woman who waits
A moment to collect her dignity
Beside the bleached bone in the terminal ward.
As she rises sobbing from the monstrous land
Stretching for milk-familiar comforting,
She will find me and between us two
It will not come. It will not come.

Foghorns

When Catrin was a small child
She thought the foghorn moaning
Far out at sea was the sad
Solitary voice of the moon

Journeying to England.
She heard it warn, 'Moon, Moon',
As it worked the Channel, trading
Weather like rags and bones.

Tonight, after the still sun
And the silent heat, as haze
Became rain and weighed glistening
In brimful leaves, and the last bus
Splashes and fades with a soft
Wave-sound, the foghorns moan, moon-
Lonely and the dry lawns drink.
This dimmed moon, calling still,
Hauls sea-rags through the streets.

The Hare
(i.m. Frances Horovitz 1938-1983)

That March night I remember how we heard
a baby crying in a neighbouring room
but found him sleeping quietly in his cot.

The others went to bed and we sat late
talking of children and the men we loved.
You thought you'd like another child. 'Too late,'

you said. And we fell silent, thought a while
of yours with his copper hair and mine,
a grown daughter and sons.

Then, that joke we shared, our phases of the moon.
'Sisterly lunacy' I said. You liked
the phrase. It became ours. Different

as earth and air, yet in one trace that week
we towed the calends like boats reining
the oceans of the world at the full moon.

Suddenly from the fields we heard again
a baby cry, and standing at the door
listened for minutes, eyes and ears soon used

to the night. It was cold. In the east
the river made a breath of shining sound.
The cattle in the field were shadow black.

A cow coughed. Some slept, and some pulled grass.
I could smell blossom from the blackthorn
and see their thorny crowns against the sky.

And then again, a sharp cry from the hill.
'A hare' we said together, not speaking
of fox or trap that held it in a lock

of terrible darkness. Both admitted
next day to lying guilty hours awake
at the crying of the hare. You told me

of sleeping at last in the jaws of a bad dream.
'I saw all the suffering of the world
in a single moment. Then I heard

a voice say "But this is nothing, nothing
to the mental pain".' I couldn't speak of it.
I thought about your dream as you lay ill.

In the last heavy nights before full moon,
when its face seems sorrowful and broken,
I look through binoculars. Its seas flower

like clouds over water, it wears its craters
like silver rings. Even in dying you
menstruated as a woman in health

considering to have a child or no.
When they hand me insults or little hurts
and I'm on fire with my arguments

at your great distance you can calm me still.
Your dream, my sleeplessness, the cattle
asleep under a full moon,

and out there
the dumb and stiffening body of the hare.

Overheard in County Sligo

I married a man from County Roscommon
and I live at the back of beyond
with a field of cows and a yard of hens
and six white geese on the pond.

At my door's a square of yellow corn
caught up by its corners and shaken,
and the road runs down through the open gate
and freedom's there for the taking.

I had thought to work on the Abbey stage
or have my name in a book,
to see my thought on the printed page,
or still the crowd with a look.

But I turn to fold the breakfast cloth
and to polish the lustre and brass,
to order and dust the tumbled rooms
and find my face in the glass.

I ought to feel I'm a happy woman
for I lie in the lap of the land,
and I married a man from County Roscommon
and I live at the back of beyond.

Windmill

On the stillest day
not enough breath to rock the hedge
it smashes the low sun to smithereens.

Quicker than branch to find a thread of air
that'll tow a gale off the Atlantic
by way of Lundy, Irish Sea.

At night it knocks stars from their perches
and casts a rhythmic beating of the moon
into my room in bright blades.

It kneels into the wind-race
and slaps black air to foam.
Helping to lower and lift it again

I feel it thrash in dark water
drumming with winds from the Americas
to run through my fingers' circle

holding the earth's breath.

Neighbours

That spring was late. We watched the sky
and studied charts for shouldering isobars.
Birds were late to pair. Crows drank from the lamb's eye.

Over Finland small birds fell: song-thrushes
steering north, smudged signatures on light,
migrating warblers, nightingales.

Wing-beats failed over fjords, each lung a sip of gall.
Children were warned of their dangerous beauty.
Milk was spilt in Poland. Each quarrel

the blowback from some old story,
a mouthful of bitter air from the Ukraine
brought by the wind out of its box of sorrows.

This spring a lamb sips caesium on a Welsh hill.
A child, lifting her face to drink the rain,
takes into her blood the poisoned arrow.

Now we are all neighbourly, each little town
in Europe twinned to Chernobyl, each heart
with the burnt fireman, the child on the Moscow train.

In the democracy of the virus and the toxin
we wait. We watch for bird migrations,
one bird returning with green in its voice,

glasnost,
golau glas,
a first break of blue.

Note: *golau glas* blue light

Lament

For the green turtle with her pulsing burden,
in search of the breeding ground.
For her eggs laid in their nest of sickness.

For the cormorant in his funeral silk,
the veil of iridescence on the sand,
the shadow on the sea.

For the ocean's lap with its mortal stain.
For Ahmed at the closed border.
For the soldier in his uniform of fire.

For the gunsmith and the armourer,
the boy fusilier who joined for the company,
the farmer's sons, in it for the music.

For the hook-beaked turtles,
the dugong and the dolphin,
the whale struck dumb by the missile's thunder.

For the tern, the gull and the restless wader,
the long migrations and the slow dying,
the veiled sun and the stink of anger.

For the burnt earth and the sun put out,
the scalded ocean and the blazing well.
For vengeance, and the ashes of language.

No Hands

War-planes have been at it all day long
shaking the world, strung air
humming like pianos when children bang the keys

over and over; willow warbler song
and jet planes; lads high on speed up there
in a mindless thrum; down here a brake of trees

churns to a rolling wave and there's no let
in the after-quiver along air-waves struck
by silly boys who think they strum guitars,

who skim the fields like surfboards over crests
of hedges, where a tractor swims in a green wake
of grass dust tossed to dry under sun and stars:

boy scaring boy off the face of his own land,
all do and dare, and look at me, no hands.

JOHN POWELL WARD
London Welsh v. Bridgend

Then I got on the train, very late
at night, Saturday, and lay on the seat,
exhausted, as did the other man
there, a little man, beady-eyed and
with a pointed chin, and he pulled the
blinds down, and we lay, and just about
dozed off when bam! door opened,
in came half a rugby team, enormous
fellows, tipped me off the seat on the
filthy floor, then sat down, singing,
shouting, crashing on each other with
their beer cans, and one sat by the
beady man, running his fingers exquisitely
along the fellow's thigh-bone, through
his trousers, but in only a bawdy
way, friendly even, if you could believe
it, and they roughed, and one
arse in the corridor, undid the fire
extinguisher, soaked us, and another
slammed the door, sat down again, kept
asking me the beady man's name, which
I didn't know, angry now, afraid even,
but decided to be sensible, and got
going, talked, had their beer, and they
got serious to meet me, a most
generous gesture, and a big man, older
than the others, kept deflecting the
attention, of the bawdy one from the
beady one, the bawdy one trying to make
the beady one talk, which he couldn't,
in inhibition, and cringing fear, and I

felt sorry, but leant on the carriage arm,
with them, drinking, singing, yawning, and
hearing about his wife, from one of them,
till, at last, they were quieter, they had
won their match, they had had a good day,
and they dozed off, one on my shoulder, sixteen
stone, snoring loudly, but I finally dozed
off, at the train's rhythm, rattling
through the darkness, and I half-woke,
at times, saw a mist scene, as of Arthur's
knights, assembled, swaying, brief white
faces, then dozed, felt the train stop
in my half-asleep condition, and men get
out, a shrieking porter, and banging doors,
then slept again, and then woke, two
hundred miles from London, they had
all gone, every one, bar the beady one, and I
sat, heavy, soggy, wanting lukewarm tea, and
saw, with my round eye and my mind's eye,
the aftermath of dawn, and the mess of the
twentieth century; the industry, the steel
works and the smelting works, a new day, for
better or worse in our hands, and the
carriage window, filthy, but a filter,
for that streaky, watery, nearly
light-blue, blue.

Here, Home

I got home, very late, and parked the
car, by the hedge, and entered the porch,
and was turning the key, when I heard a
single fox bark, a mile away, and I went
inside, put down my suitcase, and spread
my fingers on the wall to find the light-
switch, and one bulb lit dimly, and the
terrier, lying on the carpet, opened one
eye, after a second's pause, and then, a
little later, he seemed, gradually, to be
moving, and raising himself, on rear legs
only, and then the front, with an effort,
and then walked, extremely slowly, about five

steps, to me, where his nose stopped, barely
a quarter-inch, from my trouser-leg, where
he stood, in a kind of acknowledgement, as
it were, and my fingertips touched his wire
head, and I heard, a very tiny breathing, as
of two small people, perhaps, and at the top,
of the stairs, a bedroom door, half-opened,
yielded a cot, with a still form, what I
knew to be, tousled sheets, and one half of
a small, curly head of hair, exposed, like
an object I perceived, or was expert on,
and a little body, under the sheets which
went up, and then back, so carefully, and
I walked, still with my overcoat, on, along
the passage, past another bedroom, in which
a bigger boy slept, and a further door,
also, was open, to its bedroom, where a
wife lay, in black pyjamas, asleep, the
face loaded, very full, but pre-empted for
the night, and by her, in the double bed,
was a space, the shape and size of a man,
into which I climbed, fitting it, exactly,
and lay half-asleep, templating it, or would
seem so, to a further fox or man who arrived.

Marathon

In rain, two hundred runners streaming
Past us yet so out of reach
It felt they or ourselves were dreaming.
Stirred, we drove ahead to watch
And parked. The hazels dripped. A man
Tore by at murderous cold speed,
Dead silent, pounding on the road.

Second and third ran powerfully.
Groups next with oddly awkward gait,
Their minds obsessed with healthful flight.
Then masses bunched and talkative
As amateurs, at play for love.
Then stragglers in threes and twos
And ones, mud splashing round their toes.

Later, through wheat, the thin white line
Far off, slow prisoners in a chain.
Earth's low flameless fire, their motion
Rhythmic as a crescent ocean.
In from the wet they took their showers,
Towelled, dressed, then out for home rejoined
Long marathons of crawling cars.

The Wye Below Bredwardine

The banks are steep. Drought. Water too low.
Too many trees by it too, it feels. Yet
They impress heavily, this hot calm day.
Trees hang and bulge over, and peer right down.
Thirsty alders lean over, the bane of water.

Huge plate-glass windows sliding along
Horizontally, slowly rotate as they go. No
Hurry in such drift. And when flies and seeds
Hit it, dartboards widen and meet the dead
Hauteur of the banks, their raw nettle clumps.

Lower down these panes bump submerged reefs,
Lazily give, yet resist quite breaking.
Little folds and pleats adjust the Wye's surface.
Leaning over you see its tiny corkscrewings,
Like pocks on estuary mud, but down water.

Suddenly, near one bank in a patch of weedy
Sunlight, a blue shoal of chub. And,
Several feet down by the bridge's piles, one
Salmon flickered deep like a neon light.
Swinging on a branch, a tyre half-submerged.

What ease has this tonnage of sedately moving
Water. Sleepily it stirs, then enfolded
With so slight a turn rolls over in bed and
Weighs sideways down again. A hundred metres
Wide. Leaves, bubbles, downy stuff, flies.

It is evening sunlight. Already. Lambs baa.
I love you sylvan Wye, or would do so,

If that were tenable, correct, and still allowed.
Instead, I say too many trees. Traherne himself
Imagined this heaven. Is there hope? Swans arrive.

MEIC STEPHENS
Hooters

Night after night from my small bed
I heard the hooters blowing up and down the cwm:
Lewis Merthyr, Albion, Nantgarw, Ty-draw —
these were the familiar banshees of my boyhood.

For each shift they hooted, not a night
without the high moan that kept me from sleep;
often, as my father beyond the thin wall
rumbled like the turbines he drove at work, I

stood for hours by the box-room window,
listening. The dogs of Annwn barked for me then,
Trystan called without hope to Esyllt
across the black waters. Ai, it was their wail

I heard that night a Heinkel flew up
the Taff and its last bomb fell on our village;
we huddled under the cwtsh, making
beasts against the candle's light until the sky

was clear once more, and the hooters
sounded. I remember too how their special din
brought ambulances to the pit yard,
the masked men coming up the shaft with corpses

gutted by fire; then, as the big cars
moved down the blinded row on the way to Glyntaf,
all the hooters for twenty miles about
began to swell, a great hymn grieving the heart.

Years ago that was. I had forgotten
the hooters: my disasters, these days, are less
spectacular. We live now in this city:
our house is large, detached and behind fences.

I sleep easily, but waking tonight
found the same desolate clangour in my ears
that from an old and sunken level
used to chill me as a boy — the inevitable hooter

that paralyses with its mute alarm.
How long I have been standing at this window,
a man in the grown dark, only my wife
knows as I make for her white side, shivering.

Elegy for Llywelyn Humphries

Liquor, wages, automobiles, women, dope —
your gang ran all the rackets in town.
Chicago your sweet moll, Al Capone your boss,
as in the old films with grin and gun
you swaggered through the glittering twenties.

This morning, picking up a magazine, I
happen to come across your obituary: death
at seventy-six in San Quentin's hospital,
quietly, delivered by the cop cancer.
The photo shows you prosperous and gentle,

like a priest or grandfather, the scars
a boxer's perhaps but surely no killer's.
How strange then to discover that, in your day,
you swindled the state of a cool million,
sent your kid brother to the chair

and, these last years in the penitentiary,
read books on bees and economics; still more,
that your family was known to be Welsh —
farmers from some remote and derelict bro
sweating for a new deal in America.

Ah, Llywelyn, you were one of us, man!
I recognise you now and all your crooked kind:
small timers, fugitives from your people's past,
you got on in the big-shot world, but
had to face that most solitary music in the end.

So take it easy when I can't help wondering
who you might have been, with a name like that
and such remarkable enterprise, if only
you had crowed here in your own back yard.
Druan, I mourn a hoodlum, my compatriot.

JOHN BARNIE
I Had Climbed the Long Slope

I had climbed the long slope of the spur from Capel Madog to
　Banc-y-Darren
Where the hedgerows of blackthorn leaning away from the
　western wind
Thin out to be replaced by stiff fence-posts of weathered wood
That are always grey, strung with rusted barbed wire, for the
　last few miles.
On the field banks with their thin feathers of upland grass,
　harebells raised soft blue flowers
And bushes of gorse the rough intense green of their canopies.
Nobody walked here, and a wheatear ahead of me had a
　moorland tameness,
Flitting along fence-posts as I came, with its rich buff-and-grey,
　black mask, black wings and tail.
On either side parallel ridges were grouped in rough lines and
　to the north
Cader Idris was a grey wash rugged with bulk.
In the summer light the sea's geometric plane canted up to the
　horizon where
So indistinct the eyes strained to believe them, the hills of Pen
　Llŷn
Were islands, a rubbing of deeper blues between sky and water.
On the highest point of the ridge I'd stopped to look back, then
　turned
To the six houses of Banc-y-Darren strung at the throat
Of my ridge and the next, where I'd make my descent.
Out of the hills beyond, a speck hurtled ahead of itself,
A Phantom, nose tearing through the silk and pressure of the air.
In such a still world the eye follows anything that moves.
On across the valley parallel to where I stood,
It was beautiful as a harebell or a wheatear.

As it reached me, it was still ahead of its sound, as if its power
   were silence
Fuelled by the land its shadow fled across.
I could see the tanks slung under the wings
And the two grey missiles
Slim and leaning at the end of the tightened leash.
And through the clear canopy I saw Cader Idris beyond
And that the Phantom was empty.
Then the power of the engine buckled and crumpled the air,
Sound chasing this marvel which sped ahead in perfection.
It diminished to a spot until I knew it must be over the sea,
And when my sight felt that almost it must snap
And that now I could see it and now not, the Phantom fell in
   the slowest of curves,
Its fuel tanks exhausted.
The earth around me had absorbed the shock of the engine
And now in the sea there was a short white punctuation
That rose to a silent spume, then settled back
In the canted water.
The wheatear still flicked ahead of me from fence to fence
And I walked on to Banc-y-Darren
Past the few mountain ash that every year
Try out leaves above branches and trunks
That will never be more than crippled in the poor soil of these
   fields.
And I passed, on either side of the lane,
Houses with names and ordinariness,
Flowerbeds and cars, the modernized cottage and the picture-
   window bungalow,
Everything as it ought to be, yet right and not right,
As if, though there would be deaths, there would also be days
People living here would call 'tomorrow', with confidence.

The Town Where I Was Born

The town where I was born is surrounded by hills.
When the evening sky shone turquoise in summer, with small
   ribs of cloud,
And Venus wobbling its brilliance on the horizon,
The hills became solid black without any depth.
Even a farm light gave no perspective, or the lamps of a car
Bumping up to a flash then disappearing

As it twisted down a lane between banks and trees.
And when the night was grey with cloud from the Llangattock
    Mountains
To the Black Mountains across the Usk,
The hills were muggy and insecure, withdrawn without feature,
Except over the Blorenge where the under-surface of cloud had
    a reddish tinge
From the flaring of blast-furnaces in the town beyond.
There was a steady glow, with occasional flickering, like a colour
    of silence,
And I had to strain to think of the roar and shouts
As liquid steel trundled overhead in cauldrons on chains
To be poured with a shower of sparks in moulds
By men who moved quickly in the heat and glare.
Now things are different: I am another man and look at other
    hills.
Last night I stood on the doorstep after dark and stared into
    the east as if it were the past.
I could guess where Craig-y-Pistyll plunged down
And where was Bryn Garw among the invisible folds,
But all was embedded in dark. I thought: it is without and within,
Watching a car on the long track from Banc-y-Darren
Travel down through Cefn Llwyd, faltering lights that rose to a
    glare,
As if they were looking for something.
This time the cloud glowed too, and because the wind had
    veered through the day from south to east,
I could smell them burning, Birmingham and Coventry,
And the red glowering of the sky was the reflection of their
    flames,
And across Pumlumon, Liverpool and Manchester, and across
    Mynydd Epynt,
Cardiff and Bristol. The cloud slid steadily above me
And on the wind there was the smell of the fine dust of bricks
And the black dust of charcoal, and the grey dust of stones.
I never knew before how the smell of cities burning
Is like the must and acridity of old houses and the lives they
    have given up.
I remembered how in Cardiff after the war, we passed rows of
    façades
And nothing else standing, and how in a second-floor window
    for a year

There was a wine-glass intact, missed by the blast,
Placed there by the hand which had drained it and moved away
With a shining clarity, a salute and goodbye.

GLADYS MARY COLES
The Dornier
(A Farmer's Story)

The moorland blazing and a bomber's moon
lit skies light as a June dawn,
the harvest stubble to a guilty flush.
I saw from the farmhouse the smoking plane
like a giant bat in a sideways dive,
fuel spewing from its underbelly.
I remember how one wing tipped our trees
tearing the screen of pines like lace,
flipping over, flimsy as my balsa models.
It shattered on the pasture, killing sheep,
ripping the fence where the shot fox hung.
Dad let me look next morning at the wreck —
it lay in two halves like a broken wasp,
nose nestled in the ground, blades
of the propellers bent ...
I thought I saw them moving
in the wind.

If the Invader comes, the leaflet said,
Do not give a German anything. Do not tell him
anything. Hide your food and bicycles.
Hide your maps ... But these Luftwaffe men
were dead. Their machine, a carcass
cordoned off. A museum dinosaur.
Don't go nearer. Do not touch.

Trophies, I took — a section of the tail
(our collie found it dangling in the hedge),
pieces of perspex like thin ice on the grass,
some swapped for shrapnel down at school
(how strangely it burned in a slow green flame).
Inscribed *September 1940, Nantglyn,*

the black-crossed relic now hangs on our wall.
My son lifts it down, asks questions
I can't answer.

Yesterday, turning the far meadow for new drains,
our blades hit three marrows, huge and hard,
stuffed with High Explosive — the Dornier's final gift.
Cordoned off, they're photographed, defused.
I take my son to see the empty crater,
the imprint of their shapes still in the soil —
shadows that turn up time.

Heron in the Alyn

I follow the river, heron-seeking
where weed and nettle reign,
caught in my sorrows
and my imagined sorrows.
Flies flick and rise, torment
slow cattle. Willows trail the water
and floating celandine; maybe also Ophelia,
singing 'O, *you must wear your rue
with a difference.*'

Seeking the heron
I make unexpected finds —
the sludge of a water-rat's lair,
sheep's wool a ragged veil on wire,
a tree-wound colonised by fungus —
and suddenly I see the secret bird!

Hidden in a tanglebend,
grey visitant in fish-vigil,
alert in the afternoon heat.
Such startled lift-off
of great wings, crashing
through boughs, attaining sky.

I watch the slow pulse
of its flight, the laboured ease,
diminishing into distance
with its weight of unseen freight —
my sorrows, my imagined sorrows.

ANN DRYSDALE
Language Difficulty

Welsh is a mad language; there are no words in it.
Not words as Anglo-Saxons understand them.
Definite, finished words that stand for things.
Words purpose-built and unequivocal.
English has words. Ten times as many words
As there are things for them to be names for.
In Welsh it's more a case of things per word;
Pick one from the few in the dictionary —
Pwll: it's "a pit, a pool, a hole, a lake"
And you fight with the Celtic vacillation
Needing to know which, beating your stiff brain
Into a compromise — perhaps *pwll* is the darkness
That is bounded by pitness and lakeness;
Maybe the spirit of the depth itself,
A deep, dark damp, filling an emptiness.

To study Welsh is like embracing Buddhism,
Seeing the world outwith the things in it.
Glas is both 'blue' and 'green'. The Saxon spirit
Howls for a certainty. One or the other!
Who says the two are incompatible?
Certainly not the sea; I asked it once.

Once I worked late into the night, searching
For words that would stand up and take the weight
Of the great sadness that comes to me sometimes,
Into the hole left by the sort of joy
We used to know in childhood — *'Mark my words —
You carry on like that and there'll be tears
Before bedtime.'* The hurt of missing something
You never knew you had till it was gone.
Sadness for sadness' sake. Tears on a taut face
Still stretched from too much laughter. Welsh has it;
Simple as stocking-stitch, easy as breathing —
Listen: inhale — *hwyl*; exhale — *hiraeth*.

Lament of the White Queen

I was a pawn when we began this. I bowed to your black majesty,
Creeping quietly forward in the service of my king.

I asked no more then than to use my simple skills
For his especial safety. I slipped sideways sometimes
Boldened by love, to tilt at your knights and your castles
In his dear defence. His eyes were on you then
Across the great distance, the impassable terrain
Where I dodged in safety, beneath your majesty's contempt.

Far out on the battlefield, I heard that his consort had fallen:
Yet it was a surprise, I swear, when I outwitted your black
      infantry
And fortune crowned me. Feeling my power I flew straight to
      his side;
He leaned unknowing on my strength. Fulfilled, I did not
      threaten you
Preferring instead simply to defend my new and happy state,
My gentle king.

                      I saw you move and felt the world shift.
Sweeping unmarked across the chequered wastelands, you have
      set yourself
Once again in the direct line of my king's vision; he sees only you.
You are too big and cast too long a shadow towards the broken
      ranks
Of our citadel. I shall make the gesture that is now required of me,
Playing a queen's part to the end. I shall go in peace without
      pleading
For what I had for only so short a time. The day is yours.

Eheu! Eheu! Shah mat. The king is dead.

CHRISTINE EVANS
Callers

It is always a shock when they take off their caps,
Those neighbouring farmers who call at our house.
They have to, of course, to have something to roll
Or to press or to twist in their blunt nervous hands;
But it makes them instantly vulnerable
With their soft bald spots or thinning forelocks.
They seem at once smaller, and much more vivid:
Leaping out of type to personality.

The smell of their beasts comes in with them,
Faint as the breath of growing things in summer,
Rich, as the days draw in, with cake and hay and dung.
They are ill at ease in the house:
One feels they would like to stamp and snort,
Looking sideways, but have been trained out of it —
As with leaving mucky boots beside the door.

Only small, swarthy men with the friendly smell on them;
Yet walls press close and the room seems cluttered.
I am glad to go and make obligatory tea
As their voices sway, slow with the seasons,
And, ponderously, come to the point.

Lucy's Bones

Most of our bodies will melt
letting all they ever were leak out.
Between the fires and the fresh ruins
folds of white fat
hiss and gutter till flesh flows;
but her bones will arch in the earth
not gently flexed as if in sleep
but sound as boat-staves, seasoned
timber that takes two generations to give way.

Mole-mouthed as a lover
rot will move over her
a charge of blue seed
quivering her thighs, flooding
the bright, packed silks, the slit reefs
prying under fingernails
disentangling white stalks
for the petals to fall free
and alchemise to a stencil.

Then her long bones will be
galleries of sighing
her ribcage a cathedral.
The wings of her shoulders
go on promising horizons, her pelvis
pause at the edge of its double question

the little carpal and the tarsal bones
lie orderly, arranged like pieces
waiting to clatter into prophecy.

The shell of her skull shall brim with honey:
in each eye-cave a chrysalis
stir toward the shrouded sun.
Ladybird and velvet mite and leaf beetle
seedpearls of snails' eggs
nest in the sockets of her knuckles.
In each dry crack, a patient germ:
primrose and birch and rosemary,
white roots of fern to weave a launchpad.

She should be lodged in topmost branches
stirred at the heart of her own green storm
but her smile will shine out
through blinded ground, through deafened wind
because she stayed eager all her life
kept her face to the edge
constantly spending
and was charged with such brightness
waste cannot claim her.

Enlli
(for Ceri when she was ten)

We get to it through troughs and rainbows

falling and flying

rocked in an eggshell
over drowned mountain ranges.

The island swings towards us, slowly.

We slide in on an oiled keel.
Step ashore with birth-wet, wind-red faces
wiping the salt from our eyes
and notice sudden, welling
quiet, and how here the breeze
lets smells of growing things

settle and grow warm, a host of presences
drowsing, too fine-winged to see.

A green track, lined with meadowsweet.
Stone houses, ramparts to the weather.
Small fields that run all one way
to the sea, inviting feet
to make new paths to their own
discovered places.

After supper, lamplight
soft as the sheen of buttercups
and candle-shadow blossoming
bold on the bedroom wall.

Outside's a swirl of black and silver.
The lighthouse swings its white bird round
as if one day it will let go
the string, and let
the loosed light fly
back to its roost with the calling stars.

JOHN DAVIES
How To Write Anglo-Welsh Poetry

It's not too late I suppose ...
You could sound a Last Post or two
and if you can get away with saying
what's been said, then do.

First, apologise for not being able
to speak Welsh. Go on: apologise.
Being Anglo-*any*thing is really tough;
any gaps you can fill with sighs.

And get some roots, juggle names like
Taliesin and ap Gwilym, weave
A Cymric web. It doesn't matter what
they wrote; look, let's not be naive.

Now you can go on about the past
being more real than the present —
you've read your early R.S. Thomas,
you know where Welsh Wales went.

Spray place-names around. Caernarfon.
Cwmtwrch. Have, perhaps, a Swansea
sun marooned in Glamorgan's troubled
skies; even the weather's Welsh, see.

But a mining town is best, of course,
for impact, and you'll know what to say
about Valley Characters, the heart's dust
and the rest. Read it all up anyway.

A quick reference to *cynghanedd*
always goes down well; girls are cariad;
myth is in; exile, defeat, hills ...
almost anything Welsh and sad.

Style now. Nothing fancy: write
all your messages as prose then chop
them up — it's how deeply red and green
they bleed that counts. Right, stop.

That's it, you've finished for now —
just brush the poems down: dead, fluffed
things but your own almost. Get
them mounted in magazines. Or stuffed.

Sunny Prestatyn

Each day I see them carefully grow old and feed
      behind that glass, those plants,
in an aquarium's stillness — saw at first their need
      for aloneness like a niche.
It is not a need. Lured by sun-crossed memories
      of August, most have retired
from industrial towns at last to find the sea
      sucked out of reach.

They have left the wet streets that flow
         on northern towns like tides,
those separately secret worlds that tow
         forever in their wake
lives bound by the going and returning they inhabit,
         for this quiet place
where silent mornings on the daylight hours sit.
         Here no tide will break.

Some watch the sand, the blank sea stretching out, going
         endlessly nowhere.
Past bungalows, an empty paper bag goes yachting
         down the empty street.
Cars pass; seagulls stream on white safaris to the sea.
         Like their bungalows,
the old here are detached, with no shared memory
         to sift or curse or greet.

And if they had known of this, would they have stayed
         where home and friends
still were, where the family was once, and made
         the most of their discharge?
Anywhere, lack of interest, change and age itself condemn
         them, left on some beach
or trapped in tanks. We are accused of them
         and they are us writ large.

In Port Talbot

By now it's like returning to a foreign town, especially
at night when the steelworks' odd familiar fever
flushes again faint red on walls and ceilings.
Its reverberations, too, this time I cannot hear
as silence. When cars stop smashing rain to spray
or after a train has dragged its chains across stone floors
what remains is this, work's dying murmur.

Lying flat, the whole town breathes through stacks;
gouts of asthmatic coughing churn the sky.
All night in burnt air, an enormous radio
aglow with coiled circuits, aerials straining high,
blasts out selections from Smoke at ranked streets

with floatings of thick chords that echo for miles.
They drown, almost, the groundswell hum nearby.

Homes of the well-off on Pentyla have the best view
of the steelworks. The main road follows it obediently.
Running coastwards greased by rain, streets skidded
to this edge, finding metal had replaced the sea
with slabs that rear white-ridged with steam then stop.
All night, rolling in over the beached town
are breakers never seen, a thrumming like memory.

Look out on winter's thin streets. See how steel
lights up the whole town still. Although it shivers now
in November dreaming of steel's breaking point, its people —
kept from clean air but not each other — could tell how
common purpose, gathering, runs strongest
on hardest ground. As here where the land turned
overnight to metal, where smoke blooms in the window.

And when at last shared work's vibrations cease,
sharing itself will fade (as in the mining villages nearby)
with Keir Hardie's dream, with Bethanias long since ghosts,
down history's shaft. Difference and indifference will untie
taut bonds of work that cramp yet forged here a community;
then old South Wales will have to start a New. Meanwhile
reverberations still, slow leavings, long goodbye.

The Visitor's Book, 8

To swerve from village chapel to a town's
high-stepping church is, in midfield caught,
to feel life-forces collide, one woodbrown
and squat, all Welsh (my father must have thought
I'd catch faith like the measles), that tall other
dazzling in a blonde-haired surge of incense
with etiquette's deft sidesteps my mother
introduced me to. Pity, I made no sense
of either. And announcements — usually
in Ostrich — from the pulpit's grandstand failed
to clear up the game's essential mystery.
Even now I am not sure what I've missed.
From bare boards, sudden, to brass altar rail:
it's partly the shock has kept me atheist.

The Visitor's Book, 9

The TV set, stirring itself, confides
in my father in Welsh. Bored, I can see
outside the steelworks signal in the sky
to streets speaking pure industry.

His first language I did not inherit,
a stream my father casually diverted
to Cymmer clean past us all. Brisk shifts
of my mother's tongue worked in my head.

My wife and daughter speak it, strumming
on green places, a running water-beat
beyond me. But though I've picked up some
of the words, they do not sound like mine.
It is like hearing what might have been.
Pointless to mourn that far-off rippling shine.

DUNCAN BUSH
The Hook

1.
I named it sickle. But he
uses it, the old man, and he called it:
the hook.

No longer new; a flatter curve
of blade than the gold on red: crescent
of an ellipse;

and implement, not emblem:
dull, rust oiled with usage; nicked, the
harshened silver edge.

But a tool perfects, almost
like nature, more stringent than art: millennia
winnowed to this

shape since Egypt was
the world's grainhouse, longer:
a moon-edge

cutting finer than a straight:
grass, not flesh: only the point would embed,
opening an enemy

like a full sack, or the edge hack
a limb, the swung fist past its mark;
but savage enough

a symbol of agronomy
for rising serfs. The crossed hammer beat
this out blue once

in a man's fist; but mass
produced now for a dwindling few, this tool,
this weapon:

the steel flattened, arched, made
keen, even the white ash turned smooth, and
ferruled, by machine.

But finely weighted, this one:
light, as if I hefted only a handle, even
to the left hand,

even as it learns the backsweep.
I stooped and swung; the wristy, ambidextral hook
slew grass,

forestroke and back. I think
no eye bought this, but wrist: by balanced weight,
like grain;

and that is beautiful only
now, for the coarse use that refined it,
like the sea-stone.

2.
Beautiful too is the word:
swathe. I laid low all afternoon tall, green,
slender seeded grasses

of more elegance than poplars.
Their stems fell sheaved after the stroke
like armfuls of bluebells,

the blade was wet with sap.
Doubled I stooped, climbing the field
all the hot afternoon

for these red stigmata,
skinned blisters on the mounts of
both white palms.

Pneumoconiosis

This is The Dust:

black diamond dust.

I had thirty years in it, boy,
a laughing red mouth
coming up to spit smuts black
into a handkerchief.

But it's had forty years
in me now:
so fine
you could inhale it
through a gag.
I'll die with it now.
It's in me,
like my blued scars.

But I try not to think about it.

       I take things pretty easy, these days;
one step at a time.
Especially the stairs.
I try not to think about it.

I saw my own brother: rising,
dying in panic, gasping
worse than a hooked
carp drowning in air.
Every breath was his last
till the last.

I try not to think about it.

But
know me by my slow step,
   the occasional little cough, involuntary
and delicate as a consumptive's,

and my lung full of budgerigars.

Summer 1984

Summer of strike and drought,
of miners' pickets standing on blond verges,
of food parcels and

hosepipe bans ... And as (or so
the newspapers reported it) five rainless
months somewhere disclosed

an archaeology of long-evicted
dwellings on a valley-floor, the reservoir
which drowned them

having slowly shrunk towards
a pond between crazed banks, the silted
houses still erect,

even, apparently, a dusty
bridge of stone you might still walk
across revealed intact

in that dry air, a thing not seen
for years; just so (though this the papers
did not say)

the weeks and months of strike saw
slowly and concurrently emerge in shabby
river-valleys in South Wales

— in Yorkshire too, and Durham,
Kent and Ayrshire — villages no longer
aggregates of dwellings

privatised by television, but
communities again, the rented videos and tapes
back in the shop,

fridge-freezers going back
— so little to put in them anyway — and
meetings, meetings in their place,

in workmen's clubs and miners' welfare
halls, just as it had been once, communities
beleaguered but the closer,

the intenser for it, with resources
now distributed to need, and organised to last,
the dancefloors stacked

with foodstuffs like a dockside, as if
an atavistic common memory, an inheritance
perhaps long thought romantic,

like the old men's proud and bitter
tales of 1926, was now being learnt again,
in grandchildren and

great-grandchildren of their bloodline:
a defiance and a unity which even sixty years
of almost being discounted never broke.

Aquarium du Trocadéro

Here, in the terraced
gardens under the Musée de l'Homme
the stupefied,
reluctant fish stir behind glass.

The giant eel
swims 2 or 3 years
to reach the shallows
of its native river —

undulant, undinal
arrow of its unintelligible yearning,

it swallowed the Atlantic Ocean
through the slow
pulse at the gills.

Coiled like the Serpent
now in its illuminated, underwater tree
it is sleeping or dead.

The elvers
wave like weed. Born
in the tank, are they
incapable of memory or desire?

They mouth
the mollusc in the womb of rock,
like leeches.
The world blurs at the window.
They are at the source.

At other windows, tiny perch
hang
motionless,
like mobiles in the airless water,

and the sullen rainbow trout swerve
listless circuits
of their circulated tank.

The ferocious, brindled
pike cruise.

They have the neurasthenic, mad grin
and the water-cooled nervous system
of the Hollywood killer.
Here they dull like the fish in a case.

The fronts of the lighted tanks
are like Cinemascope screens in the dim light.

Lugubrious sunfish steer
towards the glass.

Found in the Garonne or the Pacific
currents, taken

from the cold Humboldt or the warm Gulf Stream,
the amnesiac, doped fish wait.

Survivors of the Flood,
their boredom is cold-blooded
and absolute.
They are in their element.

The Sunday The Power Went Off

In a darkening house we sat,
room-light gone, television shrunk
mid-shout to a speck then

nothing, even the old fridge's
whir and periodic
judder stilled,

and saw each other in
flashlit instants while
my five-year-old elder son

counted the sulphur-violet
dimness and I with him:
One. Two. Three. Four. Five:

a second for each year
of his life, and the sum for every
mile as slowly the storm

moved off to a horizon
of rumbles from that sudden
crack in the sky that seemed

right over the roof-ridge
like a rifle-shot amplifying
down a badlands canyon

in movies, the one-off, perfect shot
bringing a man unexpectedly down
forever, though the sunlight

unimpaired, the reel
unfinished, the shocked wildlife
listening a second more then

resuming its tiny business
of survival, even the dead man's
riderless skewbald reaching down to

browse the seeding grass.
Storms now scare me almost more than
my half-scared, half-excited kids,

if only for that first, premonitory
skyquake, distant and dull
as a range of hills or

that dark low cloud like hills
you get at dusk; or for that
faint first flash I know

may any time come before a roar
as of wind and of whirlwind,
finding me sitting

in this same stone house or bending
in the sunlit garden, knowing
instantly under clear air

this wasn't lightning, seeing
wife, sons, sunlight suddenly
reversed, as in a negative,

and simply waiting with them there,
too scared this time to count.

Living In Real Times
Summer, 1993

In Queen St., Cardiff, I halt to watch in a choice
of screens an over of the Trent Bridge Test,
Shane Warne looping wristspin in at
some tailender doomed at best to time-serving

till stumps. Between padded-off balls the eye flickers
to the other channel banked in
other sets, headlines unspooling soundless
beyond Curry's window, the newsreader's mouthings:

a street elsewhere foreshortened
by the long lens. Someone running in the tottering
apologetic way the very frightened run,
as if to panic and sprint could only serve

unfailingly to draw the sniper's bullet. Now
someone whom that bullet has already found. He lies
sprawled amid the usual crazed, cradling women
like one adored at last beyond all dreams.

Sarajevo? Mostar? Vukovar?... TV's intimate and
generalising eye makes everywhere somewhere else:
a province of that small, remote country
of which we, famously, know little

still. While post-modernism makes all things
present, all things post-reality (from the intensity
of this particular and very private grief I realise
I saw these shots two hours ago). Again

the street, down which no doubt the dead man too
had run. Past those same bins, the burned-out
truck, between the building's cover and
a water standpipe. Running partway

then throwing his hands up at it all
and falling dead just at that piece of broken kerb ....
As he falls over and over again now in the women's
keening, or in some syndicated twenty-second

filmclip replayed over the next day's news.
Night-time, street, streetlight, a chemist's shop,
wrote Alexander Blok as Russia came apart
(that is, the first time round):

whatever you come to, wherever
you go, it all comes down at last

to this. *You'll die, and just as always start
the dance again.* Over and over. And forever

and for ever. No *Amen.* While from the other end,
on another set, Merv Hughes — that moustache
bigger than Nietzsche's — takes the wicket,
a jubilant slip hurling high the catch, fieldsmen

throwing up their hands, the hangdog batsman
turning away, reluctant as a stood-up groom:
live now, sudden, in real time.
And I wait automatically, lingering

to watch them all do it again, in slowmo,
almost missing it the first time,
trained to the instant replay and the freezeframe:
to the destined fact, knowing there's no way out.

Brigitte Bardot In Grangetown

Off Ferry Road, the toilet of a garage where
the mechanics come at lunch to cut the hands' grease
with green Swarfega jelly, glancing once

at themselves in the rust-foxed mirror, and then
go in to eat brought sandwiches and play
pontoon with the soft, soiled pack,

three walls of the cubicle sporting the odd grey
newsprint pin-up, some *Kay* or *Tracy*,
alike as playing cards,

and then a whole closed door facing you (if
ever you sat over the stained bowl)
of Bardot as she was at twenty,

and thirty-five, and is now, in her smiling
puppy-fat fifties, still corn-blonde,
and then more of her

again (with one of Ian Rush) out where they eat,
over the workbench's oil and
hacksaw-dust, the clenched vice.

The boy who put all hers up was a six-month
Government trainee. A bit simple, they all thought.
A headbanger, the fat one said.

He had a thing about her, the boy, grinning
foolishly, half-proudly, when they kidded him, told him
she was old enough to be

his mother. *That slag?* the fat one said once.
*Look at her. She's anybody's. Even saving baby seals
all she knows how to do*

is lie down with one. And laughed: soft, smirched face
looking at that photo, then at the one of her
naked, hands raised as if to pin or

loose her hair, the honey-hued still-teenage
body, milky Mediterranean behind her, evening.
He left the other week,

the trainee. He didn't finish, he never even came
back for his tools. So now they're
anybody's like the photos:

like, the fat one knows, the photos always are.

TONY CURTIS
Preparations

In the valley there is an order to these things:
Chapel suits and the morning shift called off.
She takes the bus to Pontypridd to buy black,
But the men alone proceed to the grave,
Neighbours, his butties, and the funeral regulars.
The women are left in the house; they bustle
Around the widow with a hushed, furious
Energy that keeps grief out of the hour.

She holds to the kitchen, concerned with sandwiches.
It is a ham-bone big as a man's arm and the meat
Folds over richly from her knife. A daughter sits
Watching butter swim in its dish before the fire.
The best china laid precisely across the new tablecloth:
They wait. They count the places over and over like a rosary.

To My Father

Bellringing was another
of the things you didn't teach me.

How many crooked ladders did we climb?
How many belfries did we crouch in?
The musty smell of the years in the wood beams,
the giant domes balanced to move
against a man's pull.
Stories of jammed trapdoors and madness
in the deafening that draws blood.
Once you rang for the Queen
and I watched
all that pomp ooze into the cold stone of the cathedral.

I wanted to take the smooth grip of a rope
and lean my weight into it.
I wanted timing.
I wanted you to teach me
to teach my son's son.

Turning your back on that
brings our line down. What
have you left me? What sense
of the past? I could have lost myself in the mosaic
of Grandsires, Trebles and Bobs,
moved to that clipped calling of the changes.

I know now the churchbells' coming over the folded
town's Sunday sleep carries me close to tears,
the noise of worship and weddings and death
rolling out
filling the hollow of my throat.

Games With My Daughter

The first clear afternoon of Spring bursts
April's buds and bulbs in the park.
This year, when I catch and take her weight,
she powers the swing and arcs
from finger-stretch behind my head
to soaring feet-in-the-clouds.
Mothers to our left and right
shrink in their corridors of safe flight.

Our game's revealed the filling out,
the firmer, young woman's stare,
the promise Winter concealed beneath its coat.
Forward and up she splits the sky, each
swing down and back she goes by to where
my tip-toed fingers' grasp can't reach.

Pembrokeshire Buzzards

The buzzards of my boyhood days are back again,
their wide-stretched, ragged wings
like distant, emblematic kites. Our speed brings
them close to, still as icons, precisely drawn.

A single blown buzzard's egg nested in Pwllcrochan
at the centre of gull, wren and blackbird
in my shotgun-toting cousin's collection,
coffined in the shoe-box under his bed.

For twenty years since then, in my middle time,
they were rare. It seemed they had gone too
the way of the plagued rabbits. The oily spew
of the refineries, the tourists' fumes

and farmers' chemicals had seen them off. But
now the buzzards of my growing years are back.
Each road, every deep, high-hedged track
is reigned over by a pair — imperious, vigilant.

Where did they go? All these years.
Somewhere unseen, perched high in pylons, poles and trees
their clawed, bobbing weight was riding always.
Above our speeding car, memories lift off the wires.

Queen's Tears

In ten years, not once have these colours shown.
Inherited with our house
then relegated to my college room,
its dull green-margined petals
have filled my window space for two years.
And now *Billbergia Windii*, Queen's Tears,
sends five tendrils out with five pink sepals,
each unclenching a pendant of flowers,
blue and yellow and red.

I inherited the room, too. David,
tall and balding, fiftyish, worked here —
incongruous suit and acting pumps,
an English voice that could be powerful or plum.
It's four years since he died. A Fulbright
to California did for him —
long afternoons cruising for lovers in the sun,
anonymous bath-house couplings at night.

He sat in the office as they phoned the doctor.
I saw him there, shaking with the sweats,
his slack mouth caked with saliva.
His mind had gone beyond us. Staring ahead
he knew what was plain for us to see.

He had no family. At the funeral, actress
friends from his drama school days
did something from Proust, a Donne sonnet
beautifully read, to an audience
of colleagues and dutiful boss.

Another spring is due, the magnolia tree
knocks against the window. My first floor
view frames an angle of buildings
and the sky's parade of clouds behind
the failing Queen's Tears.

David, let the deep green, loud red
and ice blue sing for you
and all the casual folk I never really knew,
but think of on occasions, remotely, from the past,
as now. Brief flowerings that come
unannounced, and do not last.

Portrait of the Painter Hans Theo Richter and his wife Gisela in Dresden, 1933

This is the perfect moment of love —
Her arm around his neck,
Holding a rose.

Her wisps of yellow hair
The light turns gold.
Her face is the moon to his earth.

Otto's studio wall glows
With the warm wheat glow
Of the loving couple.

This is after the dark etchings,
The blown faces. This is after Bapaume —
The sickly greens, the fallen browns.

She is a tree, her neck a swan's curved to him.
His hands enclose her left hand
Like folded wings.

This is before the fire-storm,
Before the black wind,
The city turned to broken teeth.

It is she who holds the rose to him,
Theo's eyes which lower in contentment
To the surgeon's smock he wears for painting.

This is the perfect moment,
The painted moment
She will not survive.

This is before the hair that flames,
The face that chars. This is before
Her long arms blacken like winter boughs.

This is the harvest of their love,
It is summer in the soul,
The moment they have made together.

From Otto's window the sounds of the day —
The baker's boy calling, a neighbour's wireless
playing marches and then a speech.

Soup

One night our block leader set a competition:
two bowls of soup to the best teller of a tale.
That whole evening the hut filled with words —
tales from the old countries
of wolves and children,
potions and love-sick herders,
stupid woodsmen and crafty villagers.
Apple-blossom snowed from blue skies,
orphans discovered themselves royal.
Tales of greed and heroes and cunning survival,
soldiers of the Empires, the Church, the Reich.

And when they turned to me
I could not speak,
sunk in the horror of that place,
my throat a corridor of bones, my eyes
and nostrils clogged with self-pity.
'Speak,' they said, 'everyone has a story to tell.'
And so I closed my eyes and said:
I have no hunger for your bowls of soup, you see
I have just risen from the Shabbat meal —
my father has filled our glasses with wine,
bread has been broken, the maid has served fish.
Grandfather has sung, tears in his eyes, the old songs.
My mother holds her glass by the stem, lifts
it to her mouth, the red glow reflecting on her throat.
I go to her side and she kisses me for bed.
My grandfather's kiss is rough and soft like an apricot.
The sheets on my bed are crisp and flat
like the leaves of a book ...

I carried my prizes back to my bunk: one bowl
I hid, the other I stirred
and smelt a long time, so long
that it filled the cauldron of my head,
drowning a family of memories.

Land Army Photographs

How lumpy and warlike you all looked,
leaning against the back of a truck,
hair permed underneath headscarves;
in make-up, corduroys, with long woollen socks
— the uniform completed by a khaki shirt and tie.

You are posed in a harvest field:
long wooden rakes and open necks in one
of those hot wartime summers. Fifteen of you
squinting into the camera,
and the weaselly Welsh farmer, arms folded,
his cap set at an angle
that would be jaunty for anyone else.
He's sitting there in the middle, not really
knowing about Hitler, or wanting to know,
but glad to have all those girls
with their English accents and their laughs.

Mother, how young you look, hair back, dungarees,
a man's head at your shoulder.
You girls cleared scrub-land, burned gorse,
eyes weeping as the smoke blew back;
milked cows and watched pigs slaughtered.
You, who could not drive,
drove tractors with spiked metal wheels, trucks.
And once, on the Tenby to Pembroke road,
along the Ridgeway, they had you working flax.
For two days only it bloomed,
the most delicate blue flowers.
Like wading into a field of water.

I see you piling the gorse. Dried spikes
flaring into silver ferns, and smoke
twisting from the piles as the wind comes in
gusts, cool from the sea, the gulls drifting
lazily on the flow.

And then,
one of them, too steady, too level, becoming
a Sunderland coasting in to Milford Haven:
over Skomer, Skokholm, Rat Island, over the deep water;
and, though you do not know it, over a man

who is smoking, scraping field potatoes
for the searchlight crew's supper,
who pulls and unpeels the rabbit they have trapped,
joints and throws it into the steaming stew,
the oil-drum perched over an open fire;
the man who looks up, the man who is my father,
watching the white belly of that flying boat
cut into the Haven.

PETER FINCH
We Can Say That

We speak the language. No.
We understand it. We say that.
The bricks of our houses
are thick with it.
We know all the songs
and the place names.
It's not foreign.
We flaunt our origin
in the big city
where most don't
know iaith y nefoedd
from Urdu.
We do.
Heol y Frenhines it says
and we can say that.
We are native.
We have status.
Cenedl heb iaith cenedl heb galon
until we have to handle it
in Penrhyndeudraeth or Pwllheli
where, using English slyly,
we say that we're glad it isn't dead.

The Tattoo

At the ferro-concrete bike sheds
I pass a love-note to Veronica.
I wear long trousers and brylcream now

but her only interest is proven prowess.
I tattoo her name on my arm in Quink
with a penknife and show her.
She is unimpressed.
She goes out with a big ted from the fifth
who pisses over bog doors when you're in there.
He wears knuckle-dusters and can make a noise like a fart
with his armpit. Everyone is scared.
At break the Head tells me
that only criminals and soldiers sport tattoos
and sends me home to remove it.
My mother refuses. There is a dispute.
Magnificently my photograph
appears in the paper. Schoolboy Banned.
Our family are resolute.

It is over when by mistake
I wash a week later
and the whole thing goes.
I return to school a hero
where after assembly Veronica smiles
and the big ted breaks my nose.

Fists

When I form a fist
the index knuckle still stings
from the red mist a year ago when
I punched a hole in the wardrobe door.

We've exchanged hangers since. Mine are
radio ariel diamonds.

Out the back are the boxes I won't
look in. Half a menu; sea shells;
kid's first shoe.

Time is in the next room, hissing like
a cistern. My fist is another fist now, of
course, the body renewed totally every
few years. Different bones, different
skin.

I pass you your junk mail. You put it
in your bin.

I walk behind people in crowds, imitating
their steps, not being me, seeing what it
is to be them.

It works occasionally, now and then. You
don't recognise me by the veg
in the supermarket.

My fist in the frozen peas. You with him.

DOUGLAS HOUSTON

Lines on a Van's Dereliction
'Farewell! thou art too dear for my possessing.'

This rust-infested cage with worn-out brakes,
Green paintwork scratched as if a demon clawed it,
Calls forth these tribute lines for old times' sake —
It's future's scrap, I simply can't afford it.
The engine's blown some seal that keeps the oil in,
The windows seem the only parts intact;
Though recently I screwed a brand-new coil in,
Such costly items will no more exact
The cash from me to keep it on the road.
Permit me now the vocative, O van,
Defeated by that last excessive load,
The tons of logs your brakes tried to withstand
In huge momentum down the mountainside;
For many thousand miles I've driven you,
A third-hand emblem of a sort of pride,
But now the year is 1982,
Your time, at thirteen years, is up I think.
In olive groves or by the sea we parked you,
Our four-wheeled bedroom-wine-bar-kitchen-sink;
On that first trip the Florence police remarked you
And towed you off for us to go your bail,
But recollection's pasta can't obscure

The fact that now your braking power's failed
We'd like a vehicle just a wee bit *newer*.
So farewell now old heap, have fun as tins.
One day within the geochronic system
Digesting contents of all rubbish bins
My big toe might encounter your third piston.
We'll render gaseous traces to the sky
While mineral satisfactions of the earth
Redistribute our atoms by and by.
Infinity's before us right from birth;
So don't take it too badly, rusty friend,
Should I dismember you to sell as parts;
Remember being doesn't simply end,
Disintegration's where the big time starts.

A Night Out

Two thousand feet above the torrent's clattering sibilance,
    Past scrambling on heather lost in mist
    Till sharp castellations of boot-prints in peat
    Repeatedly signalled the track's assurance,
Reaching the summit is a spirited trudge through cloud,

An effort in faith, with daylight's rapid fading
    Insistent on its irrevocable deadline,
    With all views down a grey obliteration
    And craggy desolation fading yards ahead,
Faith that the refuge on the top actually exists,

That there will, indeed, be a top, that this eeriness
    Of stones stained with luminescent green lichen
    Constantly nodding out of the blown mist
    Is not some interminable last landscape
With no interest in ever being interesting.

Then a dim taking-shape out on the edge of sight
    Solidifies into a squat stone building,
    Its dirty wired windows filling with night
    While a rising gale roughs up the sky
And vodka slops by torchlight into an old tin mug.

PAUL GROVES
Anniversary Soak

What kind of love is this when she
Lifts down the urn from its high place
And takes the top off gingerly
As if about to see his face,

And then rolls down her stockings as
She did that first night they were wed,
While he lay back there, bold as brass,
A bronzed young god upon the bed?

What sort of memory is kept
Alive as both the taps are turned?
That marriage day they never slept
But like two endless fuses burned.

She steps into the swirling heat,
Uncertain whether she should stoop
Or kneel; she looks down at her feet,
And tips the ashes in. The soup

That greyly laps her limbs is him,
The only man she ever craved,
The only one to keep her warm,
With whom alone she misbehaved.

The Back End of the Horse

Was it a phoney coin that let
Him be the upright part, the eyes,
For two years running? It's damned hot
And dark down there: his hips and thighs,
My forehead on his buttocks. Pain
Will gnaw my back and neck again

This pantomime. Blindly I'll shuffle,
Kicking the air — a carefree colt,
While really I begin to stifle,
Dripping with acrid beads of sweat.
The better I perform the more's
The likelihood that the applause

Gets transferred to the brainy part,
My partner in this dumb charade.
He has the conscience and the heart,
The massive teeth, the fun façade;
I have the stumbling, shambling gait,
The lifeless tail, the clumsy feet.

His mane is stroked; my rump is slapped.
His mammoth eyelashes seem coy,
Endearing; and he is adept
At smooching with the leading boy.
An ugly sister boots my rear.
Oh, which is worse: the pain or fear?

An analyst would know, I think,
Why I allow myself this pressure.
Is it a masochistic kink,
Finding in suffering some pleasure,
Euphoria in obscurity?
A man of straw. It sounds like me.

A stable relationship? Perhaps.
We need each other, fore and aft.
We do not care if other chaps
Suppose our thespianism daft.
We may not be a thoroughbred
— I may feel stupid and half dead —

But *something* makes this seem worthwhile.
Cynics could trot out Jung and Freud
To underpin their canny smile
And clarify my hopeless void.
Let them. Lost, I blunder on
Until the entertainment's done.

    not starting from the top.
I hope you did not mind me
    rising to a stop.
So this is how you find me —

    feet, decanting woes.
that creep about on wary

and mean as much as those
Words can be light and airy

or sweep it from the room.
and symbol-ridden parlance,
        the poet's sense of doom
now and then can balance

a little levity
unrelievedly serious;
        when poetry must be
I feel it's deleterious

and hardly something worse.
eliciting a snigger
        out of a page of verse,
an unfamiliar figure

a small attempt to cut
essentially it's harmless,
        and artificial, but
The project may seem charmless

On this what is your view?
a poem written backwards.
        rather than bend them to
One might be wise to lack words

while passing on his bike.
a vicar pulling faces
        perverse, perhaps, and like
Starting from the base is

Turvy-Topsy

NIGEL JENKINS
Castration

Cutting, they called it —
but for all
his noise there was no
blood, no visible hurt:

just some thing in him
halted, to change
a bull-calf to a steer.

It didn't hurt, they said
as they caught and threw them,
locked each scrotum
for a second
in the cutter's iron gums.

The next one was mine:
round the yard we
chased him, brought him
down — hooves flying —
in a slither of dung.

They sat him upright,
like a man for barbering,
and I felt
in the warmth of his purse
for the tubes.
They gave me the tongs
and with all the steel
of my arms I
squeezed them home.

They fetched me another,
said he hadn't felt a thing.

But I wouldn't play.
With all that sky-wide bawling —
    sound his throat
    was never made for —
some nerve in me was severed.
There were words about
that weren't to be trusted.

Wild cherry

Tiptoe on wall-top, head in
clouds of white blossom, I
reached for the fullest, the
flounciest sprays, I travelled
many miles to give you them.

You placed them, smiling,
in a jar on your table,
& there was beauty between us,
between us too were words,
white clouds of words ...

One of the sprays I'd kept myself,
& I'll know on what morning
you brush up the petals, you
toss out the twigs with the ashes
& empties, yesterday's news.

Shirts

She hangs out his shirts,
pins them by the tails
to the singing line.

She hangs out his shirts,
and in the pure green
that the lawn paints them
she can see her face:
I am his wife.

In the attention
of cushions, the soft
elisions of a door,
a voice, her voice
comes back to her:
he is my husband,
I am his wife.

I am the place
he returns to, his
hunger's home.
I build every day
a houseful of rooms,
of walls to enfold
the things that he loves.

She hangs out his shirts,
and the air they breathe

fills them with flight:
his gentle arms rage
flailing at the sky,
scratching and clawing
to catch up with the wind.

She hangs out his shirts:
he is her husband,
she is his wife.

Ainadamar
'Comprendí que me habían asesinado'
Federico Garcia Lorca

Give him coffee, said the general,
        plenty of coffee:
and on the road from Viznar
to Alfacar the trees were silenced,
a leathern cloud muffled the voice
        of the moon.

It was cold, and all the world
        lay huddled in mist.
Hollow at heart, too tired to sleep,
he walked out through the dawn
to be alone with himself.
Give him coffee, said the general,
        plenty of coffee ...
        In the white silence
not a leaf breathed, nothing moved
or was — until a gateway held him,
drew him in through portals of rust —
to take a seat among the weeds,
        among the statues
mouthing lost names to the leaves.

        Something there moved —
a lamb, perhaps, a tiny lamb
enkindled from the mist — and its
        movement warmed him.
Give him coffee, said the general.
        On she danced

by the dead statues, kicking dew
in their faces with her hooves of sunlight.
Coffee, said the general, black coffee:
and there burst upon the morning —
    hooves of rock,
    mouths of iron —

a gluttoned hoard of pigs
that tore at the lamb, that this
and that way ripped her like a rag
till they'd cleaned her, hoof and hide,
    from the world.

Give him coffee, said the general,
plug his arse with bullets
    for being a queer.

But on the road from Viznar
    to Alfacar
a creature of moonlight
is moving through the trees, is dancing
at the fountain of Ainadamar.
And the townspeople drink
    of singing water.

Note: Ainadamar is the Arab name for a fountain spring
near Granada, where the Spanish poet Federico Garcia
Lorca was murdered by Nationalist fascists in 1936. The
fountain, whose name means 'Fountain of Tears', used to
supply water to the gypsy quarter of Granada.

STEVE GRIFFITHS
The mines in sepia tint

A man beats his wife on the mountainside.

Their shouts pierce the copper drumskin
of the coming storm: the earth of copper
the heather, the copper sky:

everything rumbles round inside the drum.

The man in a grey suit, white-faced,
his eyes shifting fast and nervous
copper copper copper copper the woman
outraged by my witness of her beating

my warning shout as I passed
and my feet pounded the veins of copper
across country: then, poised on thin white legs,
doubtfully angry, wet hair plastered on my forehead,
sixteen, not knowing what to do.

They gave me silent, heated looks,
and I ran on.

Later, I wrote a poem about the pylons on the horizon.

Often I have written the wrong poem.

SHEENAGH PUGH
The Guest

To be in my life, it is your duty,
since you can make it better than it is.
You know I lived always untidily,
but for a week, when I had your promise
that you would be my guest some night, my room
waited in quiet order for you to come.

And if I knew you would visit my mind,
do you not think I would put some order
in that room; open it to sun and wind;
sweep where the shadows heap up in the corner?
I would be forced to alter what I am
into what I could show you without shame.

I cannot do such housework for my own sake,
only with the prospect of such a guest,
and when I am not observed, I fall back
into my old ways, and dust comes to rest.
You love what is bright; be my observer
and keep dust from it; watch me for ever.

Guys

November light drains fast; the shadowed street
is littered with old men tacked clumsily
together from worn clothes. Most have been set
to beg for their child-masters standing by,
and plead from the obedient vacancy
of painted eyes. But sometimes, from some face,
real eyes stare out, seeing and ownerless,

begging on their own account. The children watch
resentfully these rivals canvassing
for pity, interlopers on their patch ...
Apart from this, they are embarrassing;
tobacco, loneliness and spilled meths cling
about them. If they spared a thought for us,
they would expire somewhere more decorous.

But those that are of straw and sacking sewn
come to a merry death in sight of all.
Awkwardly perched, fun's focus, they take on
the shape of suffering; finally fall
among the ashes of the festival,
while children in a warlock circle turn
and clap their hands to see the old man burn.

Railway signals
(Welsh Industrial & Maritime Museum)

This is a good place for those things to wait
whose use is over. It ends a wide street
going nowhere: artery of the failing trade
whose handsome derelict buildings were left stranded
by the ebb-tide; banks, exchanges,
chandlers, all quietly minding their lost business.

Inside the museum, the old machines
wear fresh paint. They still work; piston-engines
drive nothing round, running smooth as ever,
pulleys lift air, boilers supply power
to nowhere in particular. Outside,
a pilot cutter settles in the weed

within sight of the sea. The tide's out;
between the moorings, wooden piles jut
from the mud, each bearing a railway signal.
Nothing about them is exceptional
but their place; caught out here so far
off the rails, they look a little spare,

at a loss even, but so do most
of the exhibits, for they *are* lost
in a special way. The use is gone, you see;
it isn't like Roman jewellery
or suchlike, for that could be in use
again; the owner's dead, not the purpose.

But what's here is as far obsolete
as only modern industry can get.
What it did is being better done,
or not at all. A discontinued line,
last week's Top Thirty, last year's video game.
It moves aimlessly in the same dream

as the façades of the dead businesses,
staring up the street with their empty eyes
at the new houses for the new people.
Things have moved on; things are unsentimental
like that. You can't force the world to need you,
and if it doesn't, there's nothing much to do

except wait civilly while a layer
of nostalgia distances you, like a picture
behind glass. There will be a curious grace
to your stance, out of context and purposeless
as it is; pointing the way back,
watching the litter left in the tide's track.

'Do you think we'll ever get to see Earth, sir?'

I hear they're hoping to run trips
one day, for the young and fit, of course.
I don't see much use in it myself;
there'll be any number of places
you can't land, because they're still toxic,

and even in the relatively safe bits
you won't see what it was; what it could be.
I can't fancy a tour through the ruins
of my home with a party of twenty-five
and a guide to tell me what to see.
But if you should see some beautiful thing,
some leaf, say, damascened with frost,
some iridescence on a pigeon's neck,
some stone, some curve, some clear water;
look at it as if you were made of eyes,
as if you were nothing but an eye, lidless
and tender, to be probed and scorched
by extreme light. Look at it with your skin,
with the small hairs on the back of your neck.
If it is well-shaped, look at it with your hands;
if it has fragrance, breathe it into yourself;
if it tastes sweet, put your tongue to it.
Look at it as a happening, a moment;
let nothing of it go unrecorded,
map it as if it were already passing.
Look at it with the inside of your head,
look at it for later, look at it for ever,
and look at it once for me.

Sometimes

Sometimes things don't go, after all,
from bad to worse. Some years, muscadel
faces down frost; green thrives; the crops don't fail,
sometimes a man aims high, and all goes well.

A people sometimes will step back from war;
elect an honest man; decide they care
enough, that they can't leave some stranger poor.
Some men become what they were born for.

Sometimes our best efforts do not go
amiss; sometimes we do as we meant to.
The sun will sometimes melt a field of sorrow
that seemed hard frozen: may it happen for you.

The Woodcarver of Stendal

'Judas? You want *Judas*? Look,
nobody wants Judas.' But the bishop's clerk
was businesslike, unbudging: 'We've paid
for a full set of apostles, lad,
and we're 'avin' twelve.'

Oh right, no trouble... The worst man of all time.
I stare at the harmless wood, trying to see him,
the abhorred face. How do you carve evil?
I knew I'd need more than one model
to do him from life.

Anger: veins throbbing on the thick neck
of Master Klaus, who didn't like my work.
The glint of coin in miller Martin's face
as he gives wrong weight: old Liesl, drunk and shameless,
tugging your sleeve,

offering her blotched body... Oh, my neighbours
were a great help, donating their coarse features
to my patchwork. I took the blemishes
of my kind, the worst in all of us,
to bring him alive.

But what happened then? He looks no sourer
than laughing Liesl; as honest as my old master,
who never paid me short; as sober a man
as Martin, who has eyes for no woman
but his plain wife.

Only a great sadness marks him out,
and that was mine. I scraped my heart
when I planed him. John, James, even Thomas,
they were names, nothing beside this Judas
noosed in my grief.

The Frozen Field

I saw a flat space
by a river: from the air
a jigsaw-piece. It is green
by times, and brown, and golden,

and white. When green, it gives food
to animals: when golden,
to men. Brown, it is ridged
and patterned, but when white,
a plane of evenness.

When frost touches it by night,
it turns silver: blue shadows
etch the hollows, grassblades glitter
in the grip of silence. It was
in such a place as this,
elsewhere, on the coldest night
of a cold winter, two boys
drove a car, with some difficulty,
over the frozen hummocks: parked
in the breathtaking chill, the stillness
that weighed each leaf down,
and shot each other.

It was a place I knew
years ago: I must have seen
the field, in summer maybe,
growing turnips, grazing cattle,
dotted with the white
of sheep, the blue and orange
of tents, and all the time
travelling toward one night
vast with misery; the sharp cracks,
one-two, like branches in frost,
that broke the silence.

Who knows what a field
has seen? Maldon sounds
of marsh birds, boats, the east wind.
The thin wail across the mudflats
is a heron or a gull, not Wulfmaer,
the boy who chose to die
with his king, never having guessed
how long dying could take.

And an oak lives
a long time, but a nail-hole
soon closes. Of all the oaks

at Clontarf, which is the one
where Ulf Hreda nailed one end
of a man's guts, and walked him
round and round the tree, unwinding
at every step?

The night the boys died,
their field was Maldon was Clontarf,
was Arbela, Sedgemoor, Solferino,
was every field where a moon
has risen on grass stiff
with blood, on silvered faces.
... Aughrim was so white,
they said, with young bones,
it would never need lime again:
better not to see
in the mind's eye Magenta,
that named a new dye.

It was as if the field
clenched all this in
on itself, hunched over
the pain of all young men
since time began; as if
every crop it ever bore
crowded in on it: barley, blood,
sheep, leisure, suicide,
sorrow, so much, its being
could not stay in bounds
but spilled out over space
and time, unwinding
meanings as it went.

They tangle around
the field's riddle now: *I saw a stage*
for pain, a suffering-space.
The fine mist of aloneness closed it
in the morning: at sunset
it was flooded with blood.

Thinking such things often,
we should see too much. I see
a picnic place, a playground.

My eyes half-open, I lean
against a tree; hear through the ground
children's feet chasing.
The sunlight shivers: *someone
walked over my grave.* I chew
on a stiff grassblade.

Allegiance

The skill is leaching from his hands, moment
by moment, like light through the loose weft
of an afternoon. The burnish of talent
and success, the bronze that sun left
on his taut skin is dulling, as if it were
winter with him, but it is not winter.

He is glad now of small success,
where once the best would leave him hungry.
It looked easy, but it never was:
even with skill, the shots don't come easy.
They have not come now for a long time,
and it is growing harder to see in him

what once was: is, on the odd occasion
when the grace strays across him like sunlight
over an autumn garden. But what's gone
is gone; these late rays can't kindle it.
Goodbye the fun, goodbye the fearlessness
and the endearing certainty of success

that comes of being young, and no intimate
of failure: they're on better terms now.
He has so much practice in defeat,
its gracious words, its gestures: few know how
to manage it as well. A master
of defeat, a specialist in failure.

And I would give brighter prospects a miss
to walk in the bleached leafless garden
with its sudden gleam of berries, its trees,
black and arched, its late roses half-open,
brittle with frost. There is enough to see:
what I remember here will do for me.

HILARY LLEWELLYN-WILLIAMS
Feeding the Bat

At first it was a small cold palmful,
a hunched and sorry scrap, clenched still
but for an infinitesimal buzz and tremble

as we passed it from hand to hand
half fearful that the buzzing might explode
into uncontrollable flight. So we found

a box, and a place by the stove, and scrounged
a spoonful of dogfood from the corner shop
and waited. When the scratching started

we crowded round to listen: it was alive!
Lifting it out, it seemed larger; it moved
its clever head from side to side, gave

delicate soundings. Two eyes, dark points of light
gleamed, not at all blind, and long questioning
fingers gripped mine. Whiskered like a cat

with a cat's silken cunning it consented
to be fed from the end of a stick, opened
a triangle mouth wide, and dipped and lunged

manoeuvering meatlumps in. Laughing, we squeezed
waterdrops onto its nose, to hear it sneeze
minute bat-sneezes, to watch the supple greedy

slip of a tongue flick the droplets down.
As it warmed, it got bolder, nipping our skin
with needle teeth, unfolding its tucked wings,

turning its goblin face to the window, where
milky chilled spring daylight lured
it to sudden flight, skimming at head height

a strange slow flutter, followed by a whisper
of displaced air. Awaiting a change of weather
we hung it in a bag to sleep over the stairs

and roused it for feeding. After the second day
it arched its back to be stroked, and played
a biting game, neck stretched impossibly

backwards, slyly grinning. That evening, the sun
shone. We carried it in its bag to a vacant barn
by the river. It squealed as I left it there, long

angry squeals; but I was firm. I would not
be quite a witch yet, stroking and feeding a bat
my ears tuned to its music, swooping, flitting about —

though I lean out to the buoyant dusk, for all that.

The Little Cloth

The odour of sanctity. Candles
their clear warm waxy spirits,
fresh cut blooms in paschal yellows and white,
bitter incense swung by a solemn boy,
the smell of washed Sunday bodies.

I was fifteen: I had waited a long time.

I knelt between mother and sister.
The priest moved his hands like a doll
decked out in ivory and gold for Easter.
Latin today: charmed occult syllables,
long rustling silences, the soft chink of censers,
altar boys, white lace, male mysteries.

Sleepily, I watched my own candle dip
and shrink in its fiery terrace
under the virgin's peeling plaster toes.
I hugged an unusual dragging ache, a tightness.

Sometimes I thought I might become a saint
to go into ecstasy and talk with angels;
not worry about my figure, my crop of spots,
but to live in a forest hut on wild herbs,
breathing wisdom like clean air.

The bell's small icy note
startled me back: the white moon
of the host raised up, then the chalice.
This is my blood, he said, and drank,
and wiped the cup. When that cloth is washed

(a priest once told me) the woman
must be in a state of grace
and the water not tipped down the sink
but emptied on the ground — just think of it.

My grandmother washed and washed little bloody cloths.

Ecce Panis Angelorum a woman sang
from the choir, her voice sexless and pure.
Strong vowels responded: I felt a loosing
of knots, a moist unfolding
from darkness, my chalice filled with blood

and the gold eyes of every angel turned
towards me, and I burned
with sudden grace, and my moon-Jesus rose
from the shadows and saw me. I was a saint at last —
my blood poured out for you
and for many; my new huge pride.

The soft white secret cloth
between my legs, reminded me all day.

Two Rivers

It was here, in the long red meadow,
two princes fought a battle
in old times, in the shadow
beneath this hill,
in this dark sorrel
where children roll and squeal
flattening pathways in the brushed grass.
This ridge, the high seat,
its flank woods heavy with summer —
was this where he raised his spear,
stood lightly rehearsing the blow

while the villagers swarmed below
with pop and crisps and bright-striped folding
chairs, men in tweed caps, women
in pale blue nylon housecoats,
faces pink in an unaccustomed sun?

And the one they fought for — was she
there in the crowd with her schoolfriends
pressed round her, craning for a sight
of blood? Or sitting high
as a bird, like a Carnival Queen?
Or did she stand alone with her hair down,
her fingers twisting together, down by the river
to her knees in plumes of meadowsweet?

I think she turned her face when the blow fell
and the crowd yelled and horns blared
towards the place where the two rivers meet.

Two rivers, brown and muscled, struggle
endlessly in a pool. Warm afternoons
in our own short summer, I've gone there
to skinny-dip, the shock
of water raising up gooseflesh.
Feeling the two floods not quite equally cold:
    one with a little sun in it
    one with the mountain in it
and my body between the two
touching them both, as she once used to do.

Was it here, to this shadowed pool
when the show was over,
she fled with her nine maidens
pursued by redfaced men, her triumphant lover?
Along the footpath from the post office
they ran to fetch her; but she'd flown
with her white turned face into the alder scrub
in a flurry of wings and claws.

Now they have lost her in the long
meadow; and their darkness is complete.

She flies high
here, in the woods, at night —
I've heard her thin cry, where the rivers meet.

Making Babies

The child gives her mother a drawing of Heaven.
A blank place, empty of trees
and sun and houses; just that
lumpy cloud mattress underfoot and angels
shuffling through the cirrus
with wings askew, with haloes
balanced over their heads like upturned 'O's,
like jugglers' plates at the end of their spin.
One teeters nervously, struck rigid
on round feet studded with toes.

But this is God's show, and he upstages
all others. The child imagines him
darkbearded, genial, whistling while he works.
She explains this to her mother, who sews
cross-stitches in pink and blue silks
on a dollsized creamy smock, who threads
a smile all ready, her needle poised
before she's even looked. *There's God*
the child informs her, *making babies*.
In fact it seems he could be moving house:

surrounded by boxes labelled BLOOD, BONES,
HAIR, SKIN and so on. Here are his raw
materials: the Blood Box brims.
She's drawn him in the instant of his power,
a conjuror with something up
those bulky sleeves, to flourish
with a flash and a pop! — then paeans of applause
from the stunned, golden hosts.
Her mother laughs. *You funny little girl!*
The child frowns, flushed. She knows

what's tucked beneath her mother's print
frock, what grows there; she understands
what blood is, and skin, and hair,

the speech of her heart on her pillow — but can't
translate it. How should she draw
the fat, packed world? — vivid as sleight-of-hand,
clumsy as that play about angels,
improbable as death or dinosaurs
or Heaven buzzing like a swarm of dreams
out there where anything goes.

ROBERT MINHINNICK
Short Wave

I try to tune in, but Europe's blurred voice
Becomes stranger with the movement of the dial.

All stations seem to give a fragment of
Performance, — Mozart disarmed by a fizzled
Prodigy; innumerable cliques of wordsmiths.

As the electric crackles I make believe
I am composing an avant-garde symphony,
A sound poem for a hall of idiot speech.

But behind the static are moments of sanity:
A string quartet and interesting chanteuse,
Then histrionics at a play's climax.

For some reason, a hubbub of languages
And dim music becomes more important
Than any scheduled programme. It suits

My mood perhaps, this indecipherable mayhem
Of newscasters and sopranos, and the long
Returns to electronic gibbering.

Somewhere, behind a rockband's sudden squall,
A morse message is tapped out. For a few seconds
It is clear, articulate, before melting

Into Europe's verbiage. It was not mayday.
And I twist the dial a hairsbreadth into jazz.

Surfers

September evenings they are here after work,
The light banished from the sky behind,
An industrial sunset oiling the sea.
I watch them emerge from the last wave,
Young men and girls grinning like dolphins
In their rubbers, surf-riders swept
Suddenly onto this table of dark sand
And thrift, the coastline's low moraine.

And back again to the conflict with water,
Wiping salt-stiffened hair from their eyes,
The flimsy boards pitching like driftwood
On the swell, flattening with the ebb.
Theirs, briefly, is a perilous excitement
When the current lifts them high
And they stand erect on roofs of water,
Balanced on the summit of a wave.

And there they glide, untouchable,
The moment of flight and their bodies'
Instinctive mastery lasting until
They are somersaulted into the foam
And they creep to shore exhausted,
Barefoot, wincing with the discriminate
Steps of thieves, aware perhaps
Of something they might have won, or stolen.

Sunday Morning

I choose back lanes for the pace they will impose,
    An old perspective half forgotten
Surprising me now as the world slows
With these things the broad road lacked:
    Carboys of vitriol stacked in a garage,
Orange hooks of honeysuckle gripping a wall.

Here a church window becomes an arch of light
    And the pitching of a hymn a brief
Infusion of the air. Voices, and low

Indistinguishable words, the organ's bass
    The foundation for a ritual
I trespass in, that suddenly

Intensifies the day. On the other side
    I picture them: the ranked devout
Pulling the ribbons from the black prayerbooks
And each with his or her accustomed doubt
    Submitting to a poetry
Triumphant as the church's muscular brass.

Thus Sunday morning: a gleaning
    Of its strange wisdoms. The certainty
Of hymns comes with me through a different town
Of derelict courts and gardens, a stable
    Where a vizored man beats sparks from a wheel,
An old man splitting marble in a mason's yard,

The creamy splinters falling into my mind
    Like the heavy fragments of hymns,
Then walking on, much further, this morning being Sunday.

Catching My Breath

At midnight I walk over the bailey-bridge,
The mallows waving in dark plantations
Below me at the river's edge, the finest
Paring of the moon quite red above the town.
There's nothing I can say that's praise enough.

No feeling yet, but a new perspective.
I've spent all day in the labour-ward
Listening to the women endure a rhythm
Of pain and gas and pain, the sounds from
Their own throats desperate as the cries of the newborn.

For twelve hours then, a spectator
As astonished fathers trooped out of the theatre,
Square rugby players in knife-edge blazers,
A mechanic with a sparse teenage moustache.
And all had stood where I have done

Strapped into gown and mask, watching
The beating of two hearts pencilled on endless
Tickertape, observing a woman's fury and despair
With strange dispassion. She came with a cry,
The sudden child, her skin like grapeskin,

A blue colour, the head fist-sized and punching
At the air, the long birth cable trussing her
Like flex. Now from my place on the bridge
I see the river-shingle gleam under water;
There's no feeling yet; only a place where it will be.
I lean on the parapet to catch my breath.

The Aerial

It's a town house built between the wars
Surrounded by a plot of frozen earth.
We pay each month, at night I bolt the doors,
And if this job saves money it's worth

Challenging the nerve. Winter's first snow
Is on the hills, the sea furrowed like ploughland;
I start to hate the people who below
Pass unconcerned, not knowing that I stand

On yellow chimney-stacks blackened by smoke,
Engraved with names of potteries in Stoke-
On-Trent. How laughable, the things we come to know;
Poor steeplejack, I blink back vertigo

Until at last I'm taller than the house,
The aerial turning like a weathervane
In my hands, six feet of hollow steel aimed south
And east, seeking the invisible signal.

In a room below a screen has cleared;
The world hurls images we can't escape:
I'm overwhelmed by sudden freezing vision,
A man who climbs, a searching fragile shape.

The Drinking Art

The altar of glasses behind the bar
Diminishes our talk. As if in church
The solitary men who come here
Slide to the edges of each black
Polished bench and stare at their hands.
    The landlord keeps his own counsel.

This window shows a rose and anchor
Like a sailor's tattoo embellished
In stained glass, allows only the vaguest
Illumination of floor and ceiling,
The tawny froth the pumps sometimes spew.
    And the silence settles. The silence settles

Like the yellow pinpoints of yeast
Falling through my beer, the bitter
That has built the redbrick
Into the faces of these few customers,
Lonely practitioners of the drinking art.
    Ashtrays, a slop-bucket, the fetid

Shed-urinal, all this I wondered at,
Running errands to the back-doors of pubs,
Woodbines and empty bottles in my hands.
Never become a drinking-man, my
Grandmother warned, remembering Merthyr
    And the Spanish foundrymen

Puking their guts up in the dirt streets,
The Irish running from the furnaces
To crowd their paymaster into a tavern,
Leather bags of sovereigns bouncing on his thigh.
But it is calmer here, more subtly dangerous.
    This afternoon is a suspension of life

I learn to enjoy. But now
The towel goes over the taps and I feel
The dregs in my throat. A truce has ended
And the clocks start again. Sunlight
Leaps out of the street. In his shrine of glass
    The landlord is wringing our lives dry.

The Looters

The helicopter cameras
Bring us the freeze frames.
A black sea outlines each peninsula
As snow finer than marble dust
Blurs the steeples of the spruce.
Bad weather, the wisdom goes,
Brings a community together.
Tonight the screen is a mirror
And the news is us.

At a house in Bedlinog
A drift has left its stain
Like a river in flood
Against the highest eaves.
There will be a plaque placed there soon
As if for some famous son,
While the cataract at Cwm Nash
Is a thirty foot long stalactite
Full of eyes and mouths
And the dazzling short circuits
Of a pillar of mercury.
An icicle uncirculable by three men.

Abandoned on the motorway
The container lorries are dislocated
Vertebrae. The freeze has broken
The back of our commerce
While on the farms, the snow-sieged
Estates, people return
To old technologies.

Meat is hung in double rows,
The carcasses identified
By the slashing beams.
Each one looms hugely,
Puzzling as a chrysalis
Under its silver condom of frost.
They sway like garments on a rack
When padlocks break and the freezer-
Doors swing out. It is too cold
Here to trail blood, where bread

Is frozen into breeze-blocks
And ten thousand tubes of lager
Sparkle under their ripping caul.
As flashlights zigzag up the wall
Tights turn red and tropical bronze
In each thin wallet.

The stranded drivers sleep in schools,
Their groups determined to uphold
The constitution of the snow.
Families smile through thermos-steam,
A child with her kitten, blue
As a cinder, sucking a blanket:
The usual cast of winter's news
As the commentary runs its snowplough
Through the annihilating white.

Outside, the cars are scoops
Of cumulus, and toboggans
Polish gutters in the drifts.
We never see the looters.

They move somewhere in the darkness
Through the blizzard, beyond the thin
Bright crescent of the screen,
Those people who have understood the weather
And make tomorrow's news.

She Drove a 'Seventies Plymouth

She drove a 'seventies Plymouth,
Great barge of a thing,
Chrome erosion, filler in the wing,
Rust like a sour tooth.

It was thirty below
And on Second all the stopped traffic
Was throttling out goosefeather exhaust
Thicker than the snow,

But I had to stop dead
On the sidewalk, new workboots

Rubbing a heel. And what do you know
If I'm not staring straight into the car

At this native woman, hair
A black fan under her tuke
And every fingernail painted red.
Or something I prefer. Magenta.

I eased the fit and watched her
Take out a white pencil of salve
And moisten her top lip with the care
Of a little girl colouring in.

Then the same with the bottom
Lip. Then all around in a bright
O. I could taste it myself,
That ointment. Sweet jism.

She saw me in the mirror.
I was one yard away with the tongue
Out of my boot. So what are eyes for
I'm asking. There's nothing I done wrong.

MIKE JENKINS
Survivor

They came from the arterial streets
of Dowlais, to the pill-box estate
wired to the hillside. Married
too young, for their bodies' sake.

You were, at first, a novelty
won at a fair. Then you cried
every night, dragging them from calm
of a deep sleep like a premature
birth again and again ...
until he learnt to slumber and snore
nailed by bottles to his marriage-bed.
You grew up doing the opposite
of all the examples they set.

Now you smile survival at me,
like one of those old Dowlais buildings:
the Library propped by scaffolding
(friends hold you steady).
If I looked long enough
into the archives of your mind
perhaps I'd find the reason.

The time your father's bayonet-case
came down like a truncheon
onto your mother, you couldn't hide
behind their smoke or fan the fire
any longer. You hit his helmet-head,
so he struck out and you lay
like an imitation of the dead.

Tracey — the common name belies you.
You have reclaimed the black hills
of night with your boys on stolen bikes.
The sound of their engines
worries round and round your mother
as she sits and knits alone.
Your father's in a cot
crazily shaking its bars.

A Truant

Looking down on the open-cast pit,
a black crater, with tracks coiled
like an electrical circuit,
and yellow trucks like remote-controlled toys.
Sheer cliff blasted out has given
the mountain many spasms of shock.

With biscuit tin for his companion, we meet him,
the nightwatchman. Where he lived the nettles
and bracken root out the foundation.
His words lay bare the seam below our feet,
obstinate coal which can touch men like a plague —
the moonscape recedes beneath his peaked cap.

As if there were no fences or danger signs
he invites us to enter, as if the whole mountainside
were his parlour. He tells of pensioners
trying to hide behind the winter dark
as they snuffled out lumps of coal —
let them home along the path in his own boot-prints.

'Welsh lagoons there!' he says, 'even the weeping
of the dead miners is black.' I look again
at the bush-browed ponds of pumped water,
to Aberdare in the pocket of the hills
and then at the man, out whinberry-picking,
a truant from the narrow streets of the town.

Diver-Bird

People sat up from skin-baking or shade-seeking,
children in flabby lilos stopped squall-splashing:
not a pointy snorkeller, but a diver-bird.
'Duck!' someone called, as he dipped
and disappeared underwater, emerging
liquid minutes later as no human could.
'Guillemot', I said assured, chuckling.

Grey-black, shiny as wet seaweed
his head intent for rush of a shoal,
no periscope or radar could equal
that vision: beak needling fish
leading a feathery thread up and down.
I tried to swim out, follow him,
make clicking noises to draw his attention:
he ignored my performance.

Returning home, in reference books,
I realised 'guillemot' was just as absurd.
He was elusive here as he'd been
in the bay, no silhouette fitting.
Yet I knew he'd keep re-surfacing
further and further away, stitching
more firmly because I couldn't find a name.

CHRISTOPHER MEREDITH
Christening Pot Boiler

Chamber maid
or cabin boy
passenger
room taker
true squatter
womb liner
woman filler
menses stopper
vomit causer
quasi modo
crouched at bellmouth
belly burden
bone garden
meat tumulus
homunculus
extra pulse
fish fellow
flesh hoop
human coil
vein labyrinth
amnionaut
tethered selky
potence prover
cash remover
accident-
al occupant
multiplication
and addition
love's dower
placenta flower
blanket denter
bladder squasher
snug dweller
dug sweller
milk maker
udder flooder
tum tickler
mother kicker
sleep spoiler

pot boiler
caul crammer
wind jammer
blood swimmer
gore surfer
dam buster
home breaker
mess maker
distraught squaller
future crawler,
welcome.

Plasnewydd Square

Every thing that gains a shape
harks back to this

like the blur of noise that sharpens
to the bullet of a jet,
or the dying gust that lets the pond's hem go
unruffling back to glass
where clouds' evasions yield
to certainties of light —

all wakings, makings, comings in to focus
all unwrappings, shifts to clarity from fuzz
all resolutions into shape or song
all hardenings, all crescendoes —

all these now commemorate
the certainty of what we saw,
as if some hand had turned the lens just right
so all the planet of ourself came clear,
in one another in an empty square
one city midnight when we were calmed
with being realized and realized we knew

that this was where we both were always aimed,
stared all night till the world turned round
and in each other's eyes saw home.

HUW JONES
Man Lying in a Hallway
(L.S. Lowry, ten days before he died)

That morning
even his wireless was an irritation.
After lunch at the Alma Lodge
he'd snoozed away the afternoon
in his deep green chair. Then this:

fast to the floor like a sick dog
he lay where his knees had given way;
'Wait,' he cried, 'Wait,'
as a stream of chocolate biscuits
tumbled through the letterbox.

He listened to footsteps grow louder
then fade to a nearby bus-stop.
He threw his slippers at the door,
his diary, his wallet, then his watch.
No one came.

With darkness
weasel-faced callers
grinned behind frosted glass;
figures he'd pinned onto board
came tapping from the back room.

'Can you give me tuppence?' he cried
struggling to rise,
'Can you give me tuppence?'

CATHERINE FISHER
Severn Bore

Somewhere out there the sea has shrugged its shoulders.
Grey-green masses slip, rise, gather
to a ripple and a wave, purposeful, arrowing up
arteries of the land. Brown and sinuous, supple
as an otter, nosing upstream under the arching

bridge, past Chepstow, Lydney, Berkeley where a king
screamed; Westbury, where old men
click stopwatches with grins of satisfaction;
slopping into the wellingtons of watchers,
swamping the nests of coots, splashing binoculars.
And so to Minsterworth meadows where Ivor Gurney's ghost
walks in sunlight, unforgotten; past lost
lanes, cow-trodden banks, nudging the reeds,
lifting the lank waterweed,
flooding pills, backwaters, bobbing the floats
of fishermen, the undersides of leaves and boats,
and gliding, gliding over Cotswold's flawed
reflection, the sun swelling, the blue sky scored
with ripples, fish and dragonfly, stirred
by the drip and cloop of oars; and finally, unheard,
washing into the backstreets of the town to lie
at the foot of the high
cathedral, prostrate, breathless,
pilgrim from a far place;
refugee
from the ominous petulance of the sea.

Those Who Make Paths

Here's a song of praise for all those people
who live at the forgotten edge of things;
who come out at night and take long walks
under the lamp-posts, remembering;
women who stay behind to clean old churches,
rubbing the shining faces week by week,
speaking their thoughts to angels and the dead,
a silent congregation at their back.

Men who go out in the early morning
to gather sticks from urban river banks;
old men with allotments, or with bikes
piled with panniers of spuds;
women who push home-made carts or carry
wood on prams, grandchildren riding high
and sucking kaylee. Where are they
in the world's eye?

And those who make the paths that run through hedges,
through the corners of fields, who leave charred
sticks and charcoal deep in hidden copses;
kids who dream in corners of the yard;
anglers, and cyclists going nowhere really
but away, happy to be alone;
those who live beneath the world's dignity;
those who've been poets, and have never known.

Frozen Tarn

Some queen has left her mirror on the grass.
If I could pick it up the back
would be metal, the chased whorl and counter-whorl,
all the mystic twisting.

She's left it tilted, reflecting
the dark fringe of trees
and the grey huddle of hills.
Her mirror holds the only empty spaces.

One of those women from the ancient tales
— the tragic, defiant ones —
always with a witty answer on their tongues
and usually some secret in a tower room.

A cold oval of myth on the winter hillside,
and you, far down there
bending over, stepping out on her polished treachery,
balanced on a moving iron cloud.

Words

They are stones
shaped to the hand.
Fling them accurately.

They are horses.
Bridle them;
they'll run away with you.

They are windows,
opening on vistas
that are unreachable.

They are apples.
Bite on hardness
to the sweet core.

They are coracles;
flimsy,
soon overloaded.

They are candles.
Carry them carefully.
They have burned cities.

OLIVER REYNOLDS
from *Tone Poem*
Eous

'Undress me! Undress me!' you said
dancing with your arms out like wings,
tiddly and giggly till you flopped over me:
'Undress me.'

I wound my hand
into the end of the belt
hanging down by your side:
'Just like a tail.'

In bed my fingers planed down soft
on soft of thigh and calf
till they came to your heel's roughness,
hard as the beginnings of a hoof.

Bestiary

Python-coils of leg and trunk
confuse the hand:
where do I stop and you begin?

That thumb-size hare
we saw in the Egyptian Gallery
had your stretched-back neck now

but not these fingers
grazing and ruminating
all over my back.

You bird-burr my name
then pigeon-pout oohs and ahs
as I grunt and root deeper.

Flopped apart,
flounders washed up
on the slab of the bed,

we gape at our groins
fresh-sprigged with dark parsley
and remember

how earlier that night
we kissed in a church doorway
as fire-engines whooped by

their lights flocking over us
the sudden flits and blues
of passerine and paradise.

Spanish Dancer
(A version of Rilke's 'Spanische Tänzerin')

Like one of those old sulphur matches,
a lucifer, self-haloed in your hand
and spurting white before it catches,
she starts and the circled crowd watches
the dance feed on itself till it's fanned

into flame, sudden and bright.

The eyes set the hair alight.
The dress burns higher and higher,
red-hot, committed to the fire

from which, rearing like startled rattlesnakes,
each naked arm clicks and shakes.

Then, as if the fire were too tight a fit,
she rolls it up and, like a skin, casts it:
contemptuous, a Grand Signior
whose slave grovelling on the floor
is the fire, still burning, not yet dead —
till she, triumph almost complete,
a smiling mask on a lifted head,
stamps it out with tiny, tidying feet.

PAUL HENRY
The Winter Wedding

You played and she sang at my wedding.
    Anyone might have been there
for all you cared. (I was hiding
    with my wife, under the stairs).

Truth is, showing off was your forte,
    in your own subservient way.
Mostly quiet, but at the right party
    half an excuse and you'd play

as you played, while she sang, at my wedding,
    as if the world owed you its ears,
your bow askew, crazily sliding
    on thin ice, across the years.

Love Birds

They rendezvous each night, at ten,
for ten minutes, behind closed eyes,
he in his cell, she in the brown rocker.
And once a fortnight, for half an hour,
their fingers form a desperate nest,
remembering the robin he'd fed
that misses him at the back door,
its freedom disorientated.

The screws must laugh at these love birds,
each week's confetti of letters,
or secretly gain faith from matching
her sentences to his.

He hears her singing *Porgi Amor*
in the difficult, unreal dawns
when the walls barge further into him
and terrible lights flash in his mind,
when the bars of his hand close tightly on
what might prove the last breath
of some precious, invisible creature.

She knows all this, waiting
in the early kitchen, lovingly timing
two cracked eggs in a saucepan.

GWYNETH LEWIS
from *Six Poems on Nothing: III*

I've made friends with nothing and have found
it is a husband. See these wedding rings?
Two eyes through which I see everything

but not as I used to. Importance leaves me cold,
as does all information that is classed as 'news'.
I like those events that the centre ignores:

small branches falling, the slow decay
of wood into humus, how a puddle's eye
silts up slowly, till, eventually,

the birds can't bathe there. I admire the edge;
the sides of roads where the ragwort blooms
low but exotic in the traffic fumes;

the scruffy ponies in a scrubland field
like bits of a jigsaw you can't complete;
the colour of rubbish in a stagnant leat.

These are rarest enjoyments, for connoisseurs
of blankness, an acquired taste,
once recognised, impossible to shake,

this thirst for the lovely commonplace.
It's offered me freedom, so I choose to stay.
And I thought my heart had been given away.

from *Welsh Espionage: XI*

So this is the man you dreamt I had betrayed.
I couldn't have saved him if I'd stayed.

He's old as his language. On his bony knees
his hands are buckled like wind-blown trees

that were straight in his youth. His eyes are dim,
brimming with water. If you talk to him

he'll mention people whom you never knew,
all in their graves. He hasn't a clue

who you are, or what it is you want
on your duty visits to Talybont.

This is how languages die — the tongue
forgetting what it knew by heart, the young

not understanding what, by rights, they should.
And vital intelligence is gone for good.

The 'No' Madonnas

For the one
who said yes,
how many
said no?

Of course,
there was
the Sumatran who refused
and then the Nubian,
then the Swede,

who shied away
from bearing the Word,
though the chance
was offered ...
a Finn, a Chinese ....
Declining politely
they carried on
with the dusting
or with its equivalent
so the question
was left
to an Indian, a Lapp,
petitioned by God
for outrageous assent,
for in sweetest closeness
all being is rent.

But those who said no
for ever knew
they were damned
to the daily
as they'd disallowed
reality's madness,
its astonishment.

So the moment passed
and the fissure closed,
an angel withdrew,
no message sent,
and the lady prepared
her adequate meal —
food of free will —
from which God
a while longer
was absent.

Sunday Park

So the world offers itself in love:
A park on a Sunday with a simple band,
oom-pah-pah under the cherry tree.
What could be more ordinary?

But time divided the music like this:
To open, an easy ball was thrown,
caught with a lunge of the skirt, a laugh,
two children (related) running around
pursued by a dog who can't get enough
of municipal smells from the mellow sound
which starts to repeat — the ball gets thrown,
till, this time, the girl runs round on her own,
followed by dog with a lolloping tongue.

Then the reprise: ball in an arc,
not fumbled now but moving free
from one hand to another, the dog, then three
youngsters (must be one family)
chased by the music; the sun goes in,
world goes flat, dog takes a break,
but the children are back, each one a repeat
with variations and, in their wake,
a blackbird bouncing as crescendo and ball
arch over the moment and let them all through,
toddler chasing the other two,
dog yapping, happy having caught a ball
in the doily shade of the cherry tree
where the baton beat out eternity
for a moment before we went home for our tea.

STEPHEN KNIGHT
The Big Parade

Here they come past High Street station, everyone I've ever known
and some I've only seen on television, marching three abreast,

my Junior School Headmistress at the front — Miss Morgan
with her bosoms now as much a shelf as when I saw her last

it must be thirty years ago — hurling to the sky a silver baton
(twirling up it tumbles earthwards like the prehistoric bone

in Kubrick's *2001*): turning at the Dizzy Angel Tattoo Studio
down Alexandra Road then into Orchard Street they go,

my other teachers — Grunter, Crow and Mister Piss on stilts —
juggle furry pencil-cases, worn board-dusters, power balls,

there's Adam West, his Batman outfit taut around his waist,
and then the Monkees, Mickey hammering a drum the others

blowing on kazoos: they navigate the Kingsway roundabout
to pass the Odeon where everyone is dropping ticker-tape

a storm of paper falls on Malcolm in a stripy tank-top, John
and Hugh and catches in the hairnet of our loony neighbour

Nestor — keeping up despite an ancient Zimmer frame —
and Bill the communist and Mister Shaddick, hirer of skips,

his brown bell-bottoms crack and snap around his platform shoes,
the collar of his paisley-patterned shirt's two giant set squares

look! a girl from Pennsylvania who kissed me once, still thirteen
after twenty years, I shouldn't recognise her smile and yet I do,

I call to her but she's too far away, atop a jewelled elephant
she's waving to the crowd like someone fresh from outer space:

travelling along St. Helen's Road towards the sea, the cheers,
the noises of the instruments resounding through the city centre

out, past vinyl three-piece suites and lava lamps in Eddershaws
go Mary Dorsett, Julie Dolphin, Tony (very much alive),

Rhiannon then a row of faces I can't put a name to now
but still I wave and shout and watch them disappear,

the boy who butted me one break-time skulking at the back,
the music fading, blurring with the gulls, the sea, the sounds

of people going home, till everywhere I look
the streets are quiet as a fall of snow.

Daedalus
for my father

The sink is choked with dirty plates,
Dead leaves, twigs — the tree
Outside the house disintegrates

But Daedalus could be
No happier now he's begun
  To build his dream. To me

The watery autumnal sun
  Is cold and yet he sings
Out loud he's having so much fun.

  Obscured by coffee rings
& marmalade, his drawings flap
  Among the breakfast things

When breezes lap
  Doors and walls, our dripping tap.

*

Although he's working with antiques
  His father owned (the saw,
Flaked with liver spots, stalls & squeaks;

  The chisel fails to score
The softest wood; nails snap or fold)
  Still, shavings crust the floor

And clouds of sawdust fall like gold
  All afternoon: drifts grow
In saucepans. Sometimes, when that old

  Paint-speckled radio
Beside the kettle plays a song
  He used to know

He sings along —
  Every other word is wrong!

*

He works all day, intent, absurd,
  Narrowing his eyes
Because his pencil marks have blurred

  ~~And~~ nothing's cut to size.
At sunset, when a sudden wind pours
  Through every room then dies

Away, he's there still, on all fours
  To improvise with string
& strips of Sellotape. Though doors

  Slam shut, though feathers cling
To him — his gluey hands, his hair,
  His clothes — he's whistling

Without a care.
  Feathers falling everywhere.

DERYN REES-JONES
Largo

Each week, our great Aunt Doris came to teach me piano,
rattling her strings of purple plastic beads, and smelling of
  carbolic,

her emerald boa draped around her like a mutilated treble clef,
her loose false teeth clacking like a metronome

as she pointed with a knitting needle to the notes of Dvořák's
  Largo
with which I soon grew bored, and played too quickly, and too
  loud.

Sometimes she'd tell me stories as I played
about the man she loved before the war, the telegram

they sent to let her know that he was killed
in action at the front. And by the end of half-an-hour

I was so proud — my fingers aching from such speed
and was left breathless. Both our eyes were full.

I never really learnt to play the piano, but for that
one inimitable tune, and not long after

great Aunt Doris died, from a tumour leaving her first
stone deaf, then blind. Years later, now, on empty afternoons

I play the *Largo* sometimes, the way that she had wanted it,
smoothly, and slowly, as if somehow those belated sounds

could compensate for all the sad percussions of her life,
the palpitating gaps, the ill-struck chords.

The Great Mutando

Pulls rabbits out of hats
Ties up the day with handkerchiefs in silk.

So many colours make me cry.
LADIES AND GENTLEMEN, FOR MY NEXT TRICK!

He spins the earth.
Blues. Greens. A plate

On a stick.
Punch. Judy.

Five silver glistening rings.
That link

Then come apart.
Six doves.

Five fly, one suffocates.
A little drop of shit runs down his sleeve.

He makes a Dachshund from three pink balloons.
Mutando!

I want a name like that.
And a world. .

Wands. Fairy Godmothers.
No crocodiles.

A place where I can get the handkerchiefs to knot.

BIOGRAPHICAL NOTES

W.H. Davies (1871-1940) was born in Newport, Monmouthshire. After leaving school, aged fourteen, he attended evening classes. At the age of twenty-two he went to the USA where he lived as a tramp. In 1899, he had an accident as a result of jumping a train and had a leg amputated. In 1905, having returned home, he published his first book of poems at his own expense. It was favourably reviewed by Edward Thomas who encouraged him to write his celebrated memoir, *The Autobiography of a Super Tramp*. During his lifetime he published twenty volumes of poetry.

Edward Thomas (1878-1917) was born in London of Welsh parentage. After leaving Lincoln College, Oxford, he resolved to earn his living through his pen. Between 1897 and 1917 he published some thirty prose volumes. It is generally believed he wrote poetry only during the last two years of his life. In fact, in his second prose book, *Beautiful Wales* (1905), the poem 'Llewellyn, the Bard' was no translation from the Welsh as Thomas pretended but one written by him. Between December 1914 and April 1917, Thomas wrote 143 poems. Thomas was killed at Arras on April 9th 1917.

A.G. Prys-Jones (1888-1987) was born at Denbigh, North Wales and educated at Pontypridd Grammar School, Llandovery College and Jesus College, Oxford. For many years he was an Inspector of Schools. His first book, *Poems for Wales* was published in 1923; his final volume *More Nonesense* in 1986. He is considered one of the few Anglo-Welsh poets to have excelled at writing funny poems.

Wilfred Owen (1893-1918) was born in Oswestry. His father reckoned the Owen family were descended from the Sheriff of Merionethshire during the reign of Henry VIII. Owen's uncle, E.G. Shaw, a Welsh International centre forward, played against Scotland and Ireland. Wilfred Owen began writing poems early, influenced by the work of John Keats. He abandoned romantic leanings to become the most acclaimed realist poet of the First World War. In October 1918 he was awarded the Military Cross only to be killed in action the following month.

David Jones (1895-1974), the poet-painter, was born at Brockley, Kent. During the First World War he served with the Royal Welsh Fusiliers. His experiences on the Western Front seeded his long poem *In Parenthesis* (1937). Earlier, in 1921, he converted to Roman Catholicism and subsequently joined Eric Gill's community of artists, first at Ditchling, then at Capel-y-ffin in Wales. His trip to Jerusalem with Gill in 1934 proved influential in his later writings: *The Anathemata* (1952) and *The Sleeping Lord and Other Fragments* (1974).

Gwyn Williams (1904-1990) was born in Port Talbot, Glamorgan. From 1935 until he retired he taught English Literature at various universities in the Middle East. In Cairo he became associated with the poets Lawrence Durrell and Bernard Spencer. His fine translations from the Welsh were published in *To Look for a Word* in 1976. His own poems were collected from four earlier volumes in 1987.

Idris Davies (1905-1953) was born in Rhymney, Monmouthsnire. At the age of fourteen he was already working in a coal mine and did so until the General Strike of 1926. Afterwards he studied at the University of Nottingham and became a schoolteacher. His first volume of poems, *Gwalia Deserta* was published in 1938. In 1943 *The Angry Summer* appeared and in 1945, *Tonypandy and Other Poems*.

Glyn Jones (1905-1995) was born in Merthyr. Most of his life he worked as a schoolteacher in Cardiff. He was a short story writer as well as a poet. And his autobiographical writings can be found in *The Dragon Has Two Tongues*. His *Collected Poems* was published posthumously in 1996 and selected writings, *Goodbye, What Were You?* in 1994.

Vernon Watkins (1906-1967) was born in Maesteg, Glamorgan. He was educated at Repton and at Magdalene College, Cambridge. His father had been a bank manager and eventually Vernon himself became a clerk at Lloyds Bank in Swansea. His first book was published in 1941. Several volumes appeared with the passing of the years, the last being *Fidelities* which was published posthumously in 1968. His *Collected Poems* appeared in 1986.

Lynette Roberts (1909-1995) was born in Argentina of partly Welsh parentage. She married Keidrych Rhys in 1939 and they made their home at Llanybri, Carmarthenshire. She was the author of *Poems* (1944) and *Gods with Stainless Ears* (1951). 'Poem from Llanybri' was probably addressed to the poet Alun Lewis.

Jean Earle (b.1909) was born in Bristol but was brought up in the Rhondda and lived for many years in various parts of Wales. Remarkably her first collection, *A Trial of Strength* did not appear until 1980, but has been followed by four more, most recently *The Sun in the West* (1995).

Brenda Chamberlain (1912-1971) who was born in Bangor, North Wales, was trained as a painter. But in 1958 she published her first and only books of poems, *The Green Heart*. The following year she moved to Bardsey (Ynys Enlli) a small island close to the tip of the Llŷn peninsula, about which she wrote poetically in a prose work, *Tide Race* (1962).

Henry Treece (1912-1966) who was of Welsh extraction was born in the West Midlands. He was associated with the New Apocalypse movement of poetry, into which he tried to draw Dylan Thomas. His books of poems include *Invitation and Warning* (1942) and *The Haunted Garden* (1947).

Michael Burn (b.1912) is a long-time resident in north Wales following distinguished careers in the army and journalism. A winner of the Keats Poetry Prize, he is a novelist, dramatist and general author in addition to publishing four volumes of poetry.

R.S. Thomas (b.1913) born in Cardiff but brought up on Anglesey before his education at Shrewsbury, UCNW Bangor and theological training at St. Michael's College, Llandaff. From the hill-farmer poems of his earlier work through nationalist politics and the theological and philosophical explorations of his current writing Thomas is an occasionally provocative but influential, almost revered figure.

Clifford Dyment (1914-1970) was born in Alfreton, Derbyshire, yet he identified himself as Welsh, having spent his youth in Caerleon, Monmouthshire. During the Second World War he wrote documentary film scripts. He was the author of seven books of verse and his *Collected Poems* was published in 1970.

Dylan Thomas (1914-1953) was born in Swansea where he went to school. Subsequently he worked for a short time as a reporter on the *South Wales Daily Post*. His first book, *Eighteen Poems* appeared when he was only twenty years of age. *Twenty-five Poems* followed in 1936, *The Map of Love* in 1939 and *Deaths and Entrances* in 1946. He was also the author of autobiographical short stories, *Portrait of the Artist as a Young Dog* (1940) and the popular play *Under Milk Wood*.

Alun Lewis (1915-1944) was born in the mining village of Cwmaman, near Aberdare in Glamorgan. He was educated at Cowbridge Grammar School and the University of Aberystwyth. His first book of poems *Raider's Dawn* (1942) appeared when he was in the army during the Second World War. His second poetry book *Ha! Ha! Among the Trumpets* was published posthumously, Lewis having died in Burma. His volumes of short stories, *The Last Inspection* and *In The Green Tree* appeared in 1942 and 1948.

Roland Mathias (b.1915) was born at Talybont-on-Usk, Breconshire. Although his father was an army chaplain, (he was educated in military schools, at Caterham and Jesus College, Oxford) Mathias was a conscientious objector in the Second World War. A teacher (later a headmaster), he co-founded and later edited *Dock Leaves* (the *Anglo-Welsh Review*) and is the author of seven volumes of poetry, most recently *A Field at Vallorcines* (1996).

Emyr Humphreys (b.1919) was born at Prestatyn. His long career as a prize-winning novelist and radio and television producer has somewhat overshadowed his work as a poet, though he has published four collections.

John Stuart Williams (b.1920) was born at Mountain Ash and educated at UC Cardiff. A teacher and lecturer, he is the author of four books of poetry, including the prize-winning *Dic Penderyn and other poems* (1970).

Harri Webb (1920-1995) was born in Swansea and educated at Magdalen College, Oxford where he read Romance Languages. After the war he worked as a librarian at Mountain Ash, Glamorgan. His first collection of poems, *The Green Desert*, was published in 1969, his second, *A Crown for Branwen* in 1974. His work was often energised by nationalist fervour.

His *Collected Poems*, edited by Meic Stephens, appeared posthumously in 1995.

Robert Morgan (1921-1994) was born in Penrhiwceiber, Glamorgan. he left school, aged fourteen, to join his father in the local colliery. Later he worked at a school for maladjusted boys in Portsmouth. During his lifetime he published five volumes of verse.

T.H. Jones (1921-1965) was born near Llanafan Fawr in Breconshire. Service in the navy interrupted a degree at UC Aberystwyth where he was also awarded an M.A. A teacher and WEA lecturer he eventually emigrated to Australia where he lectured at the University of New South Wales. He published three books of poems during his short lifetime, the last being *The Beast at the Door* (1963).

Leslie Norris (b.1921) was born near Merthyr Tydfil. Formerly a teacher, a headmaster and a college lecturer he has for many years been Visiting Professor at a number of American universities. His first book, *The Tongue of Beauty*, appeared in 1941; ten volumes later his *Collected Poems* were published in 1996. Norris is also a distinguished short story writer, and has translated Rilke.

Ruth Bidgood (b.1922) was born at Seven Sisters, Glamorgan. She read English at Oxford, served as a coder in the WRNS and later worked for *Chambers Encyclopaedia*. She returned to Wales thirty years ago to publish seven well-received collections, including a *Selected Poems* (1992). Also a local historian, her poetry is very much concerned with the landscape and community of Abergwesyn, where she lives.

John Ormond (1923-1990) was born at Dunvant near Swansea and attended Swansea University. For a time he was a journalist on *Picture Post* before joining the BBC in Wales. He made several notable documentary television films about Welsh writers and painters. His first book of mature poems appeared in 1969 — *Requiem and Celebration*. This was followed, in 1973, by *Definition of a Waterfall*. His final poems, along with much of his earlier work, were published in *Selected Poems*, 1987.

Joyce Herbert (b.1923) was born in the Rhondda and educated at UC Cardiff. Her poetry was first published in the forties but was interrupted until the seventies, when she was once again widely published. Her collection *Approaching Snow* appeared in 1983.

Dannie Abse (b.1923) was born in Cardiff and studied Medicine at Cardiff, King's College and Westminster Hospital. A poet, novelist, playwright, he has also published diaries and autobiography. He has published eleven volumes of poetry including a *Collected Poems*. The poems in this present anthology were chosen in consultation with Cary Archard, Mick Felton and Joan Abse.

Raymond Garlick (b.1926) was born in London but educated in north Wales. He taught and lectured in The Netherlands and Wales, and was the co-founder and first editor of *Dock Leaves* (the *Anglo-Welsh Review*).

A longstanding supporter of the Welsh language, his five collections of poetry are also concerned with Wales's place in European culture.

Mercer Simpson (b.1926) was born in London and educated at Cambridge. A teacher and lecturer in Wales for many years he has been tirelessly active in promoting the work of writers from Wales. His first book of poems did not appear until 1993, to be followed by *Rain from a Clear Blue Sky* a year later.

John Tripp (1927-1986) was born in Bargoed, Glamorgan. He worked for many years as a journalist in London until, in 1969, he returned to Cardiff to make a poor living as a freelance writer and poet. From 1973-1979 he was the literary editor of the Welsh magazine, *Planet*. During his lifetime some eight books of his verse appeared. A *Selected Poems* was published in 1989.

Christine Furnival (b.1931) was born in London of Welsh parents and educated at Cambridge. She has worked in advertising and adult education, and has translated from Italian in addition to writing stage and radio plays and four volumes of poetry.

Tony Conran (b.1931) was born in India but educated in north Wales, where he became a lecturer at UCNW Bangor. Much of his poetry is rooted in Welsh-language poetry, of which he is an eminent translator.

Harry Guest (b.1932) was born in Penarth and read Modern Languages at Cambridge and the Sorbonne. Following six years as a lecturer in Japan he returned to England to teach in Exeter. His poetry was first published in the 1960s.

Herbert Williams (b.1932) was born at Aberystwyth. A free-lance journalist and radio producer he has published three volumes of poetry and several books on historical subjects.

Sam Adams (b.1934) was born in Gilfach Goch, he was educated at UC Aberystwyth and was a lecturer before becoming an HMI. He is the editor of a number of books and is the author of two collections of poetry, most recently *Journeying* (1995).

Jon Dressel (b.1934) was born in St Louis, Missouri of Welsh descent. A journalist, businessman and academic, he established the study centre for American students at Trinity College, Carmarthen. Mostly resident in the US, he has published four collections in Wales, most recently *The Road to Shiloh* (1995).

Bryn Griffiths (b.1935) was born in Swansea. After a period in the Merchant Navy and work in London he emigrated to Australia. His first book, *The Mask of Pity* appeared in 1966. His sea poems were published in *The Dark Convoys* (1974).

Sally Roberts Jones (b.1935) was born in London but returned to Wales in the 1960s, documenting her family's roots in *Relative Values* (1985). Formerly a librarian she is the founding editor of Alun Books.

Gillian Clarke (b.1937) was born in Cardiff, where she read English. After a period in broadcasting in London she returned to Wales as a lecturer and writer. One of Wales's best known poets, she has also written for the stage and for children. Her *Collected Poems* appeared in 1997.

John Powell Ward (b.1937) was born at Felixstowe and educated at Hereford Cathedral School and the Universities of Toronto, Cambridge and Wales. He lectured at UC Swansea for twenty-five years, editing *Poetry Wales* during some of that period. His five collections include *Genesis* (1996); he has also published a number of critical studies.

Meic Stephens (b.1938) was born at Treforest and educated at Aberystwyth and Rennes. The founder of *Poetry Wales* and later first Literature Director of the Welsh Arts Council, he is now a university lecturer. He has edited numerous books, including *The Oxford Companion to the Literatures of Wales*, and also translates from the Welsh.

John Barnie (b.1941) was born in Abergavenny. After his degree at Birmingham he lectured at the University of Copenhagen and then for the Open University before becoming editor of *Planet*. His poetry collection *Heroes* was published in 1996; he has also published fiction and essays about the Blues, and the environment.

Gladys Mary Coles (b.1942) has a home in north Wales was educated at the Universities of Liverpool and London. A poet, editor and biographer of Mary Webb she also runs the poetry publishing house, Headland.

Ann Drysdale (b.1942) who now lives in Gwent was brought up and educated in London. A journalist and newspaper columnist in Yorkshire and Wales, her first volume of poetry was *The Turn of the Cucumber* (1995).

Christine Evans (b.1943) was born in Yorkshire but moved to her family's locale on the Llŷn peninsula in 1967. A teacher and lecturer, her four collections are marked by their lyrical and contemporary portrayal of the area.

John Davies (b.1944) was born in Cymmer and educated at UC Aberystwyth. He has taught in America and north Wales and is the author of seven books, most recently *Dirt Roads* (1997).

Duncan Bush (b.1946) was born in Cardiff and educated at the Oxford, Duke and Warwick Universities. Currently resident in Luxembourg, his poetry books have included translations from French and Italian. Also a novelist, his most recent collection was the prize-winning *Masks* (1995).

Tony Curtis (b.1946) was born in Carmarthen and educated at UC Swansea, he is currently Professor of Poetry at Glamorgan. A prize-winning poet, he has published seven collections, including *Taken for Pearls* (1993), and has edited several anthologies and critical works.

Peter Finch (b.1947) was born in Cardiff. The manager of Oriel, the specialist poetry bookshop, he is the author of several guides to small presses and poetry publishing and has published numerous books, pamphlets and tapes of his own poetry, conventional and concrete. His most recent collection is *Useful* (1997).

Douglas Houston (b.1947) was born in Cardiff and educated at the University of Hull. A literary researcher and writer, the most recent of his two collections is *The Hunters in the Snow* (1994).

Paul Groves (b.1947) was born in Gloucester and brought up in Monmouthshire. A teacher and lecturer he has published two collections of verse, *Academe* (1988) and *Menage à Trois* (1995).

Nigel Jenkins (b.1949) was born on the Gower and educated at Essex University. His books include a selected poems, *Acts of Union* (1990), and a study of Welsh missionaries in India, *Gwalia in Khasia* (1996).

Steve Griffiths (b.1949) was born on Angelsey and educated at Cambridge. He lives in London where he is a researcher in social issues. His *Selected Poems* appeared in 1993.

Sheenagh Pugh (b.1950) was born in Birmingham and read modern languages at Bristol. Her seven collections include a *Selected Poems* (1990) and *ID'S HOSPIT* (1997). She is also a gifted translator whose work was collected in *Prisoners of Transience* (1985).

Hilary Llewellyn-Williams (b.1951) was born in Kent but has lived for many years in west Wales. She has published three books, *The Tree Calendar* (1987), *Book of Shadows* (1990) and *Animaculture* (1997).

Robert Minhinnick (b.1952) was born in Neath and educated at Aberystwyth and Cardiff. An environmentalist and essayist he has written for television and two books on contemporary culture. He has published six collections of poetry, the most being *Hey Fatman* (1994).

Mike Jenkins (b.1953) was born and educated at Aberystwyth. After working abroad he now teaches in Merthyr Tydfil, and is active in politics and the popularisation of writing. His six collections include *Graffiti Narratives* (1995) which is written in local dialect. Jenkins is also the author of a book of stories for teenagers.

Christopher Meredith (b.1954) was born in Tredegar and educated at UC Aberystwyth. A university lecturer, he is also an acclaimed and award-winning novelist in addition to the author of two poetry collections, *This* (1984) and *Snaring Heaven* (1990).

Huw Jones (b.1955) was brought up in Welshpool and read Theology at UC Aberystwyth. After some years working in Africa he has returned to lecture at UCNW Bangor. His collections are *A Small Field* (1985) and *The Cockerels of Otse* (1997).

Catherine Fisher (b.1956) was born in Newport, where she still lives. A teacher, she combines writing poetry with an award-winning career as a children's novelist. Her poetry collections include *Immrama* (1988) and

The Unexplored Ocean (1994).

Oliver Reynolds (b.1957) was born in Cardiff and educated at Hull University. The author of three collections of poetry, he has also written for the stage and for children.

Paul Henry (b.1959) was born in Aberystwyth. A graduate in English and Drama and formerly a singer-songwriter, he works in the Careers Service in Cardiff. His books are *Time Pieces* (1991) and *Captive Audience* (1996).

Gwyneth Lewis (b.1959) was born in Cardiff, where she now works as a documentary film-maker. She has published two collections in Welsh as well as the English language *Parables and Faxes* (1995).

Stephen Knight (b.1960) was born in Swansea and educated at Oxford. A free-lance theatre director in London, he is the author of two collections *Flowering Limbs* (1993) and *Dream City Cinema* (1996).

Deryn Rees-Jones (b.1968) of Welsh lineage was born in Liverpool and educated in Bangor and London. She works as a lecturer at Hope University, Liverpool. Her first collection, *The Memory Tray*, was published in 1994 and was shortlisted for the Forward Poetry Prizes.

ACKNOWLEDGEMENTS

W.H. Davies: all poems from *Selected Poems* (OUP) © the Estate of W.H. Davies; **Edward Thomas**: all poems from *Collected Poems* (Faber); **A.G. Prys-Jones**: poem from *Collected Poems* (Gomer), by permission of the Estate of A.G. Prys-Jones; **Wilfred Owen**: all poems from *Collected Poems* (Chatto & Windus); **David Jones**: *In Parenthesis* and *The Sleeping Lord* are published by Faber & Faber, © the Estate of David Jones; **Gwyn Williams**: all poems from *Collected Poems 1936-1986* (Gomer), © Mrs D. Williams; **Idris Davies**: all poems from *Collected Poems* (University of Wales Press 1995), © Ceinfryn and Gwyn Morris; **Glyn Jones**: all poems from *Collected Poems* (University of Wales Press 1996), © Mrs D. Jones; **Vernon Watkins**: all poems from *Collected Poems* (Golganooza); © Mrs G. Watkins; **Lynette Roberts:** 'Poem from Llanybri' from *Poems* (Faber & Faber) © the Estate of Lynette Roberts; **Jean Earle**: 'Visiting Light', 'Jugged Hare', 'Old Tips', 'Blondie', 'Backgrounds Observed' and 'The Tea Party' are from *Selected Poems* (Seren 1989), 'Exits' and 'The May Tree' from *The Sun in the West* (Seren 1995), © Jean Earle; **Brenda Chamberlain**: poem from *The Green Heart* (OUP), © the Estate of Brenda Chamberlain; **Henry Treece**: from *The Haunted Garden* (Faber & Faber); **Michael Burn**: both poems from *Open Day and Night* (Chatto), © Michael Burn; **R.S. Thomas**: 'Welsh Landscape', 'Cynddylan on a Tractor', 'A Welsh Testament', 'On the Farm', 'The Bright Field' and 'A Marriage' from *Collected Poems* (Dent), 'Geriatric' and 'Still' from *No Truce with the Furies* (Bloodaxe), © R.S. Thomas; **Clifford Dyment**: both poems from *Collected Poems* (Dent), © the Estate of Clifford Dyment; **Dylan Thomas**: all poems from *Collected Poems* (Dent) and in America *The Poems of Dylan Thomas* (New Directions Publishing Corp.), reprinted by their kind permission and that of the Dylan Thomas Trust; **Alun Lewis**: all poems from *Collected Poems* (Seren), © Mrs G. Lewis; **Roland Mathias**: 'Porth Cwyfan' is from *Snipe's Castle* (Gomer), the other poems from *A Field at Vallorcines* (Gomer), © Roland Mathias; **Emyr Humphreys**: poem from *Ancestor Worship* (Gwasg Gee), © Emyr Humphreys; **John Stuart Williams**: 'Early Days is from *Banna Strand* (Gomer), 'The Complaint of Augustus Brackenbury is from *Aquarius* magazine, © John Stuart Williams; **Harri Webb**: all poems from *Collected Poems* (Gomer), © the Literary Estate of Harri Webb; **Robert Morgan**: 'The Blood Donor' © Robert Morgan, 1967 and printed with the permission of Mrs Jean Morgan; **T.H. Jones**: all poems from *Collected Poems* (Gomer), © the Estate of T.H. Jones; **Leslie Norris**: all poems from *Collected Poems* (Seren), © Leslie Norris; **Ruth Bidgood**: all poems from *Selected Poems* (Seren), © Ruth Bidgood; **John Ormond:** all poems from *Selected Poems* (Seren), © Mrs G. Ormond; **Joyce Herbert**: both poems from *Approaching Snow* (Poetry Wales Press 1983), © Joyce Herbert; **Dannie Abse**: 'Return to Cardiff', 'Hunt the Thimble', 'Pathology of Colours', 'In the Theatre', 'Case History' are from *White Coat, Purple Coat* (Hutchinson), 'Welsh Valley

Cinema, 1930s' from *Planet* magazine and 'Thankyou Note' from *On the Evening Road* (Hutchinson), © Dannie Abse; **Raymond Garlick**: 'Dylan Thoms at Tenby' and 'Note on the Iliad' are from *Collected Poems* (Gomer), 'Consider Kyffin' from *A Sense of Europe* (Gomer), 'Behind the Headlines' and 'The Heiress' from *Travel Notes* (Gomer), all © Raymond Garlick; **Mercer Simpson**: 'Homo Erectus Cerne Abbas' from *Rain from a Clear Blue Sky* (Gomer), © Mercer Simpson; **John Tripp**: 'The Last at Lucy's is uncollected, 'Caroline Street, Cardiff' is from *Bute Park* (Second Aeon), 'Ploughman' is from *Passing Through* (Poetry Wales Press), all other poems from *Selected Poems* (Seren), © the Estate of John Tripp; **Christine Furnival**: poem from *Towards Praising* (Triskel), © Christine Furnival; **Tony Conran**: 'Spirit Level' from *Spirit Level* (Christopher Davies), 'Elegy for the Welsh Dead' and 'Thirteen Ways of Looking at a Hoover' from *Blodeuwedd* (Poetry Wales Press), © Tony Conran; **Harry Guest**: poem from *Slow Dancer*, © Harry Guest; **Herbert Williams**: poem from *The Dinosaurs* (Triskel), © Herbert Williams; **Sam Adams**: 'Rough Boys' is taken from *Planet* magazine, 'Gwbert: Mackerel Fishing' from *The Boy Inside* (Triskel), © Sam Adams; **Jon Dressel**: 'Intercity, Swansea-London' is from *The Road to Shiloh* (Gomer), 'Let's Hear it for Goliath' is uncollected, © Jon Dressel; **Bryn Griffiths**: 'The Master' is from *The Mask of Pity* (Christopher Davies), 'Dolphins' from *The Dark Convoys* (Aquila), © Bryn Griffiths; **Sally Roberts Jones**: 'Household Cavalry' is from *Relative Values* (Poetry Wales Press), 'Another Lazarus' from *The Forgotten Country* (Gomer), © Sally Roberts Jones; **Gillian Clarke**: 'Baby-Sitting' and 'Foghorns' are from *Selected Poems* (Carcanet), 'The Hare', 'Overheard in County Sligo', 'Windmill' and 'Neighbours' are from *Letting in the Rumour* (Carcanet), 'Lament' and 'No Hands' are from *The King of Britain's Daughter*, all reprinted by permission of the author and Carcanet Press Ltd; **John Powell Ward**: 'London Welsh v. Bridgend' and 'Here, Home' are from *To Get Clear* (Poetry Wales Press), 'Marathon' and 'The Wye Below Bredwardine' from *Genesis* (Seren), © John Powell Ward; **Meic Stephens**: both poems from *Exiles All* (Triskel), © Meic Stephens; **John Barnie**: both poems from *The Confirmation* (Gomer), © John Barnie; **Gladys Mary Coles**: both poems from *The Glass Island* (Duckworth), © Gladys Mary Coles; **Ann Drysdale**: both poems from *The Turn of the Cucumber* (Peterloo Poets), © Ann Drysdale; **Christine Evans**: 'Callers' is taken from *Looking Inland* (Poetry Wales Press), 'Lucy's Bones' from *Cometary Phases* (Seren) and 'Enlli' from *Island of Dark Horses* (Seren), © Christine Evans; **John Davies**: 'How to Write Anglo-Welsh Poetry' and 'Sunny Prestatyn' are from *At the Edge of Town* (Gomer), the other poems from *The Visitor's Book* (Poetry Wales Press), © John Davies; **Duncan Bush**: 'The Hook', 'Pneumoconiosis' and 'Summer 1984' from *Salt* (Poetry Wales Press) and 'Aquarium du Trocadéro' from *Aquarium* (Poetry Wales Press, 'The Sunday The Power Went Off', 'Living in Real Times' and 'Brigitte Bardot in Grangetown' from *Masks* (Seren), © Duncan Bush; **Tony Curtis**: 'Preparations', 'To My Father', 'Soup' and 'Land Army Photographs' from

Selected Poems (Poetry Wales Press), 'Games with My Daughter' from *The Last Candles* (Seren), 'Pembrokeshire Buzzards', 'Queen's Tears' and 'Portrait of the Painter Hans Theo Richter and his Wife' from *Taken for Pearls* (Seren), © Tony Curtis; **Peter Finch**: 'We Can Say That' is taken from *Poems for Ghosts* (Seren), 'The Tattoo' from *Selected Poems* (Poetry Wales Press) and 'Fists' from *Useful* (Seren), © Peter Finch; **Douglas Houston**: 'Lines on a Van's Dereliction' is from *With the Offal Eaters* (Bloodaxe) and 'A Night Out' from *The Hunters in the Snow* (Bloodaxe) © Douglas Houston; **Paul Groves**: 'Anniversary Soak' and 'Turvy-Topsy' are from *Academe* (Poetry Wales Press), 'The Back End of the Horse' from *Ménage à Trois* (Seren), © Paul Groves; **Nigel Jenkins**: all poems from *Acts of Union* (Gomer), © Nigel Jenkins; **Steve Griffiths**: 'The Mines in Sepia Tint' from *Selected Poems* (Seren), © Steve Griffiths; **Sheenagh Pugh**: 'The Guest' is taken from *Crowded by Shadows* (Christopher Davies), 'Guys', 'Railway Signals', 'Do you think we'll ever get to see Earth, sir?', 'Sometimes' and 'The Frozen Field' from *Selected Poems* (Seren), 'The Woodcarver of Stendal' from *Id's Hospit* (Seren), 'Allegiance' from *Sing for the Taxman* (Seren), © Sheenagh Pugh; Hilary Llewellyn-Williams: 'Feeding the Bat', 'The Little Cloth' and 'Two Rivers' are taken from *Book of Shadows* (Seren), and 'Making Babies' from *Animaculture* (Seren), © Hilary Llewellyn-Williams; **Robert Minhinnick**: 'Short Wave' is taken from *A Thread in the Maze* (Christopher Davies), 'Surfers' from *The Dinosaur Park* (Poetry Wales Press), 'Sunday Morning', 'Catching my Breath' and 'The Aerial' from *Life Sentences* (Poetry Wales Press), 'The Drinking Art' from *Native Ground* (Christopher Davies), 'The Looters' from *The Looters* (Seren) and 'She Drove a 'Seventies Plymouth' from *Poetry Wales* magazine, © Robert Minhinnick; **Mike Jenkins**: 'Survivor' is taken from *Invisible Times* (Poetry Wales Press), 'A Truant' from *The Common Land* (Poetry Wales Press) and 'Diver-Bird' from *This House My Ghetto* (Seren), © Mike Jenkins; **Christopher Meredith**: 'Christening Pot Boiler' is taken from *Snaring Heaven* (Seren) and 'Plasnewydd Square' from *Poetry Wales* magazine, © Christopher Meredith; **Huw Jones**: poem taken from *The Bright Field* (Carcanet), © Huw Jones; **Catherine Fisher**: 'Severn Bore' is from *Immrama* (Poetry Wales Press), the other poems from *The Unexplored Ocean* (Seren), © Catherine Fisher; **Oliver Reynolds**: 'Tone Poem' is from *The Player Queen's Wife* (Faber & Faber) and 'Spanish Dancer' from *The Oslo Tram* (Faber & Faber) © Oliver Reynolds; **Paul Henry**: both poems from *Captive Audience* (Seren), © Paul Henry; **Gwyneth Lewis**: all poems from *Parables and Faxes* (Bloodaxe), © Gwyneth Lewis; **Stephen Knight**: both poems from *Dream City Cinema* (Bloodaxe), © Stephen Knight; **Deryn Rees-Jones**: both poems from *The Memory Tray* (Seren), © Deryn Rees-Jones.